BRODY'S REVIEW

LIVING ENVIRONMENT
2019

ENVIRONMENT REVIEW IN LESS THAN 100 PAGES

M. Brody M.A. ED

© 2019 Moshe Brody

It is forbidden by Federal and local law to copy in any format any page from this book without the express permission of the author.

For all comments and questions please email: Brodysregentreview@gmail.com

To purchase your copy:
please go to Amazon.com and search for Brody's Review

Table of Contents

Chapter 1	Life Processes	6
Chapter 2	Cells and its Parts	8
Chapter 3	Multicellular Systems	14
Chapter 4	Cell Respiration in Plants and Animals	17
Chapter 5	Enzymes	20
Chapter 6	Homeostasis	22
Chapter 7	Disease and Homeostasis	24
Chapter 8	**Reproduction** (edited and approved by Hagaon HaRav Chaim Yisroel Belsky zatza"l)	28
Chapter 9	DNA Action and Replication	34
Chapter 10	Mutations and Individuality	37
Chapter 11	Genetic Engineering and Biotechnology	41
Chapter 12	Ecology	43
Chapter 13	Relationships in an Ecosystem	47
Chapter 14	Energy Recycling	52
Chapter 15	Biodiversity and Environmental change	53
Chapter 16	Human Impact on Ecosystems	57
Chapter 17	The impact of Technology and Industrialization	62
Chapter 18	Scientific inquiry	65
Chapter 19	Laboratory skills	69
Chapter 20	Evolution (edited and approved by Hagaon HaRav Chaim Yisroel Belsky zatza"l)	76
	Answer Key	85

CHAPTER 1
Life Processes

1) What is life? There is no simple definition; however there are some basic characteristics shared by all living organisms. They all:
   a. have internal structures and are made up of one or more cells
   b. need energy to function which they acquire through various chemical reactions. The combinations of all chemical reactions are called Metabolism.
   c. maintain Homeostasis (or an internal stability) despite external environmental changes
   d. reproduce and pass down their genetic information to another generation

Life Processes

2) In addition, most living things share some basic life processes. They:
   a. obtain nutrients (food) from the environment and break them down for easy transport
   b. undergo digestion and synthesis (see # 15 below). They also break down nutrients so that they can derive the energy from them through Cell Respiration.
   c. grow in size by the increase in number or size of cells
   d. remove waste products through some type of excretion
   e. respond to external and internal stimulus

3) All living things also share some chemical properties listed below
   - 4 main elements of life: Hydrogen, Oxygen, Carbon, and Nitrogen. Most living things are made of these elements.

Organic and Inorganic Molecules

4) Organic and Inorganic Molecules
   - Organic Molecules: contain both Carbon and Hydrogen atoms and make up some of the most important molecules used by living things.
   - Inorganic Molecules: do not contain both elements of Carbon and Hydrogen but any other combination of elements (including one of these two) and which include salt, water etc.

Basic Structures

4a) The following are some basic structures found in all animals:
   - Organelles: are parts of the cell structure that carry out specific functions. They are (but not limited to) Ribosome's, Mitochondria, Vacuoles, Golgi bodies, Nucleus, Cell membrane, Cell wall (in plants), Cytoplasm, and Chlorophyll.

- **Cells:** the basic unit of life. In animals cells carry out specific functions in conjunction with other cells. In bacteria, and other similar organisms, they comprise the whole organism itself.
- **Tissues:** specialized cells grouped together, which, when combined with other tissue, create organs.
- **Organs:** tissues that group together to perform one of life's processes e.g. a kidney, a heart etc.
- **Organ System:** Organs grouped together to perform a life process such as the heart and circulatory system.

REGENTS REVIEW

1. Prions are proteins that act as an infectious agent. They cause a variety of diseases, including "Mad Cow" disease. Prions cannot produce more prions on their own, but cause the host organism to replicate more prions. Most scientists do not consider prions to be alive. A valid reason for accepting that prions are nonliving things is that:
    (1) no living thing can cause a disease
    (2) proteins are inorganic molecules
    (3) prions contain all of the material needed to reproduce
    (4) prions cannot carry out reproduction independently

2. One characteristic of all living things is that they
    (1) develop organ systems
    (2) produce identical offspring
    (3) maintain internal stability
    (4) synthesize only inorganic matter

3. The diagram below represents an activity that occurs in the human body.

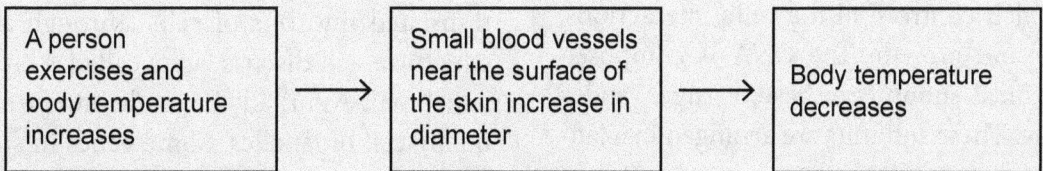

    This diagram best illustrates
    (1) active transport
    (2) maintenance of homeostasis
    (3) synthesis of nutrients
    (4) differentiation

CHAPTER 2
Cells and their Parts

5) As we have already listed the major parts of a cell, let's examine the parts of the cell in detail (see below for picture).

6) Cytoplasm: the jelly like substance in all cells that hold all the organelles in place, transport materials throughout the cell, and is the place of many chemical reactions.

7) Nucleus: is the cell's "nerve center" and also the place where the cell's DNA is stored. It is also essential in cell division (or DNA replication) and protein synthesis. The nucleus contains 23 pairs of chromosomes (or 23 molecules of DNA-each chromosome is one molecule of DNA) which controls all the cell's interactions, structure and growth. The DNA is composed of 3 chemical subunits: a base, a sugar, and a phosphate. These subunits are arranged in a ladder like structure. DNA is a complex molecule which is folded into a double Helix. (like this).

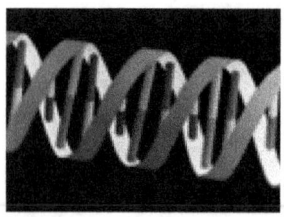

DNA is composed of 4 bases (a base is a type of chemical compound): Adenine-Thymine and Guanine-Cytosine and form base pairs called GC and AT. All these bases form the individual "rungs" of the DNA "ladder" and are part of a code which "tell" the cell how to make its cell parts. When the rungs of DNA are put together to create one instruction, it is called a Gene. For example, on the DNA there could be AT, AT, GC, AT **or** an AT, AT, AT, GC (with a GC in the fourth slot-not third). These different combinations are stacked up one on top of another with each base pair containing part of one instruction. Thus, when sections of DNA form one instruction, this is called a Gene. These instructions are translated into bits of cells (through a process which we will discuss later) called Amino acids which will eventually be made into proteins and finally cell organelles. Some genes in simple organisms are a few base pairs (rungs on the ladder), while in humans some genes are composed of up to a million base pairs! Different bases on the DNA are the reason why we have different cells, tissues, organs and ultimately why there are different species.

8) Vacuoles: are the storage tanks of the cells either holding nutrients or wastes.

9) Ribosomes: are protein producers (the place where new organelles are assembled). Sometimes these Ribosome's float and someimes are attached to membranes in the cell.

10) Mitochondria: the cells "engine" i.e. place where the food gets processed and energy exploited. These mitochondria house special enzymes used to extract energy from nutrients.

11) Chloroplasts: the green structures in plants and one celled organisms that hold Chlorophyll. Chlorophyll contains green pigments (coloring agents) that absorbs the light energy from the sun and uses it in helping the cell obtain nutrition.

12) Cell Membrane (skin of the cell):

- Separates cells from each other and
- Controls what comes in and out of cells through the use of specialized receptors on its surface. In plant (and most bacteria and fungi) an additional Cell Wall surrounds the cell membrane.
- In plants this wall helps the cells contain its structure in case the plant absorbs too much water.

Diffusion and Active Transport

There are two ways molecules move in and out of cells: Diffusion and Active transport.

13) Diffusion is a naturally occurring process whereby molecules (such as water, nutrition etc.)

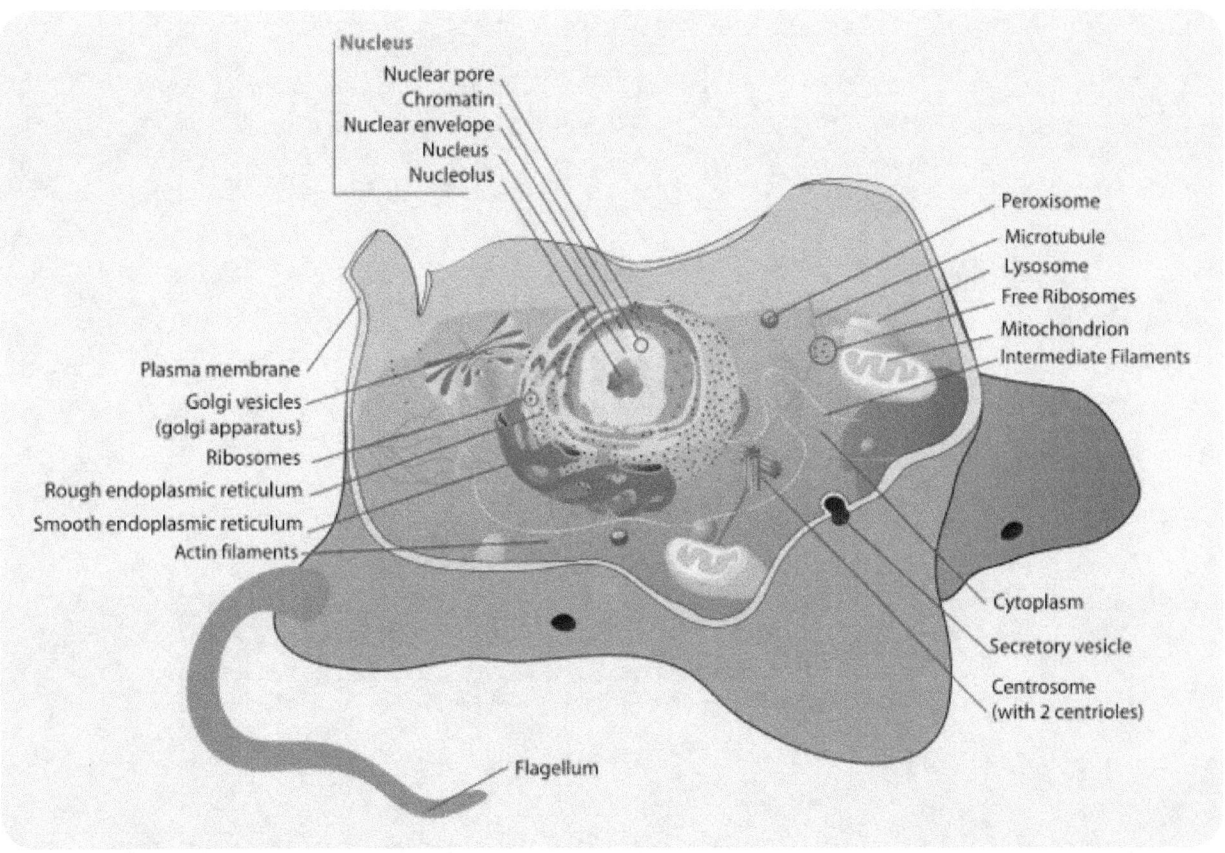

Living Environment Regents Review | 9

move from areas of higher concentrations to areas of lower concentrations by themselves. This occurs through a naturally occurring "jiggling" of the molecules and does not require energy from the cells to transport these molecules into the cell. For example, if there is a high amount of water outside the cell and a little water inside the cell, water will naturally flow through diffusion into the cell. This process helps plants absorb water from the outside, but can also cause harm to plants when they absorb too much salt from the outside.

14) Active transport: Cells use energy from ATP (high energy nutrition packets-processed in the mitochondria) to move molecules from areas of low concentration outside the cell to areas of high concentration inside the cell. (Desert plants do this in order to bring water into them where the soil has low concentrations of water compared to its roots.)

15) Sometimes molecules such as starches and proteins are too large and complex to enter the cell and thus need to be broken down into smaller amino acids (by proteins) and simple sugars (by starches). This process is called digestion. They are then reassembled inside the cell to make proteins, starches, and cell parts. This reconstruction process is called synthesis.

16) Membranes of cells have certain molecules called receptor molecules which receive communications from other cells. For ex., when hormones reach a cell from a different part of the body, the cell's receptor molecules may pick it up and this may trigger a cellular response.

REGENTS REVIEW

1. Which two cell structures work together in the process of protein synthesis?
   (1) nucleus and chloroplast
   (2) ribosome and vacuole
   (3) nucleus and ribosome
   (4) mitochondrion and cell membrane

2. The cell represented below produces oxygen.

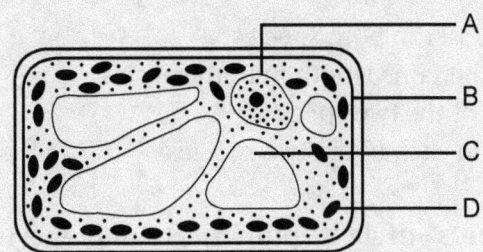

   Which structure allows the passage of this oxygen to the environment?
   (1) A
   (2) B
   (3) C
   (4) D

The diagram below represents a cell and several molecules. The number of molecules shown represents the relative concentration of the molecules inside and outside of the cell.

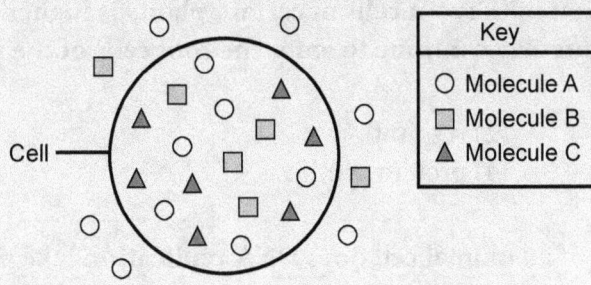

3. Molecule B could enter the cell as a direct result of
   (1) digestion
   (2) diffusion
   (3) active transport
   (4) enzyme production

4. Which two terms are considered to be opposite processes?
   (1) photosynthesis and autotrophic nutrition
   (2) cloning and mitosis
   (3) digestion and synthesis
   (4) dynamic equilibrium and homeostasis

Living Environment Regents Review | 11

5. Which sequence correctly represents the arrangement of structures containing genetic material, from the largest to the smallest size?

   (1) chromosome → gene → nucleus
   (2) nucleus → chromosome → gene
   (3) gene → chromosome → nucleus
   (4) gene → nucleus → chromosome

6. The DNA of a fly and the DNA of a gorilla are made up of subunits that are

   (1) arranged in the same order in both species
   (2) arranged in chains of the same length in both species
   (3) different bases in each of the two species
   (4) in different sequences in each of the two species

7. The colors and scents of plants attract helpful insects and repel insects that feed on them. The production of the proteins that provide these colors and scents is the direct result of the

   (1) behavior learned from parent plants
   (2) presence of specific genes
   (3) the genetic makeup of the surrounding vegetation
   (4) inability of plants to move as animals do

8. The calcium concentration in the root cells of certain plants is higher than in the surrounding soil. Calcium may continue to enter the root cells of the plant by the process of

   (1) diffusion   (2) respiration
   (3) active transport (4) protein synthesis

9. Within which structure of an animal cell does DNA replication take place?

   (1) vacuole   (2) cell membrane
   (3) nucleus   (4) ribosome

10. Plant cells can synthesize energy-rich organic molecules, and later break them down to extract that energy for performing life processes. These activities require direct interaction between the

    (1) chloroplasts and vacuoles
    (2) cell walls and ribosomes
    (3) chloroplasts and mitochondria
    (4) ribosomes and mitochondria

12. The diagram below represents cells and hormones present in the human body.
    (1) nucleus and chloroplast   (2) ribosome and vacuole
    (3) nucleus and ribosome   (4) mitochondrion and cell membrane

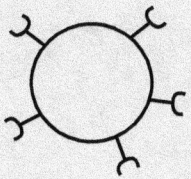
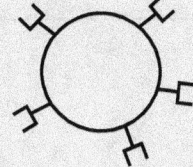

Hormone A   Hormone B   Hormone C
  ■   ▲   ●

Which statement correctly describes an interaction between the hormones and the cells?
    (1) Hormone A is synthesized by cell 2 and targets cell 1.
    (2) Hormone B bonds with both cell 1 and cell 2.
    (3) Specific reactions carried out by cell 1 are regulated by hormone C.
    (4) The specialized receptor molecules on cell 1 secrete hormone B.

13. **In a DNA sample, 15% of the bases are thymine (T). What percentage of the bases in this sample are adenine (A)?**
    (1) 15%   (2) 30%
    (3) 35%   (4) 85%

CHAPTER 3
Multicellular Systems

The Human Body

17) Digestive system: Digestion is the way food is broken down and processed throughout the body. Food enters the mouth where it is chewed (by the teeth) and broken down into small, easy-to-swallow portions and then moved down to the esophagus (a "pipe" for food) with the help of the tongue. The esophagus pushes the chewed-up food down towards the stomach through muscular contractions (called peristalsis). From there it enters the stomach-and is broken down again by acids and enzymes and then pushed into the small intestines. In the small intestines, the (now dissolved) food is absorbed into the walls of the small intestine by the way of tiny villi which line the wall of the small intestine. It should be noted though that some molecules, such as glucose, can enter the bloodstream directly without being broken down first. The dissolved food then is transported throughout the body. When food enters the cells, it releases its energy when the chemical bonds between the molecules break apart. Foods with a greater amount of chemical bonds will produce more energy. After all the extractable food is taken out, the waste is collected in the large intestine and eventually eliminated from the body.

18) Respiratory system: The Respiratory system is the system which supplies oxygen needed for the cells to produce energy from the nutrients it has absorbed (see # 2 above for more about cell respiration). Additionally, it is also responsible for getting rid of the carbon dioxide from the body which is a by-product of cell respiration. The respiratory process begins when air enters the mouth and nose (through inhaling) and heads down to the lungs through the windpipe (called the trachea). The lungs then transfer the oxygen to the heart, which pumps the oxygen throughout the body while absorbing carbon dioxide from the blood. The carbon dioxide is then transferred out of the body through a process called exhaling.

19) Circulatory system: The circulatory system carries digested food, oxygen, and water throughout the body via the blood stream. The blood also carries wastes and carbon dioxide out of the body. Additionally, the blood carries hormones (chemical messengers) and antibodies (infection fighters) to protect the body from attack. The human circulatory system includes the heart, blood vessels. There are two types of blood vessels: arteries and veins. Arteries, carry blood *away* from the heart and transport the oxygen rich blood around the body. Veins carry carbon dioxide filled blood back to the heart. Capillaries are tiny tubes of blood which branch out from arteries and veins and reach every part of the body supplying and removing blood to/from them.

20) Excretory system: The Excretory system removes waste from the body. These wastes include urine, feces and sweat as well. The organs in this system are the lungs, kidneys, and sweat glands in the skin.

21) Muscular and skeletal system: The muscular and skeletal system contains muscles, ligaments, tendons and bones which provide movement and support for the body.

22) Nervous and Endocrine system: The nervous and endocrine systems coordinate and control all the various systems of the body. They do this by either sending electrical pulses (in the case of the nervous system) throughout the body informing the body how to react, or by sending chemical messages (in the case of the endocrine system) to the cells to start or stop a process. The brain and the nerves are part of the nervous system while glands such as the pancreas, (which holds several important hormones-important also in the digestive system) testes and ovaries are part of the endocrine system.

23) Immune system: the immune system protects the body against disease. This system includes white blood cells and antibodies which protect against attack.

24) Reproductive system: the reproductive system allows the continuation of the species through the joining of the two parents' genes. The part of the body in the male that manufactures the seed materials is called the testes and that which transports the seed is called the penis. In the female the ovaries produce the eggs and the uterus contains them.

Interactions between various systems

25) There are many interactions between the various systems in the body. For example, the nutrients from the digestive system and oxygen from the respiratory system are transported through the circulatory system. Furthermore, hormones from the endocrine system regulate the reproductive system.

26) Body systems maintain homeostasis - Besides interacting, the body as a whole regulates itself so that it maintains a certain homeostasis or stability. For example, when the body gets cold, it starts a process called shivering which is controlled by the nervous system in order to heat itself up. Another example is where hormones are released when blood sugar levels go too high in order that the body does not go into diabetic shock.

Humans and other organisms: comparisons and contrasts

27) Comparisons: Humans have a lot in common with other mammals. We are generally made up of the four main elements mentioned in chapter one, and have similar cells and organs like blood, nerves, muscle etc. Additionally, our organ systems are very similar. (They have digestive systems and circulatory systems and so do we.) In addition, our reproductive systems are similar and we all have DNA. **Contrasts:** our mental capacities are unique and far exceed that of any other animal.

REGENTS REVIEW

1. Which molecule can diffuse from the digestive tract into the human bloodstream without first being digested?
   (1) protein   (2) starch
   (3) starch   (4) glucose

2. The nucleus of a cell coordinates processes and activities that take place in the cell. Which two systems perform a similar function in the human body?
   (1) nervous and endocrine
   (2) digestive and reproductive
   (3) circulatory and respiratory
   (4) skeletal and muscular

3. More energy can be released from a fat molecule than from a glucose molecule because the fat molecule contains more
   (1) genes   (2) organic compounds
   (3) chemical bonds (4) mitochondria

4. Which substance can enter a cell by diffusion without having to be digested?
   (1) water   (2) protein
   (3) starch   (4) fat

A single-celled organism is represented below.

5. Structure X carries out a function most similar to which structure in a human?
   (1) lung   (2) brain
   (3) ovary   (4) heart

6. In the diagram below, which letter indicates the part of the cell that carries out a function most similar to a function of the human excretory system?
   (1) A   (2) B
   (3) C   (4) D

16 | Living Environment Regents Review

CHAPTER 4
Cell Respiration in Plants and Animals

Photosynthesis

28) Photosynthesis is a process whereby a plant draws on solar energy and converts that energy (using water H20 and carbon dioxide-CO2) into chemical energy (glucose) which it uses as its basis for its sustenance. The part of the plant cell responsible for capturing that sunlight and converting it to energy is called the chloroplast. When photosynthesis is complete, glucose (a type of sugar) and other organic compounds are obtained. Plants use this glucose to make ATP (fuel for itself) through a process called cell respiration. Besides breaking down the glucose, plants synthesize the glucose and use it as a building block for complex molecules such as starch needed by the plants. A byproduct of photosynthesis is oxygen. Thus, plants take in carbon dioxide and give off oxygen in an exchange called the Gas Exchange. In humans and animals, carbon dioxide is released and oxygen is obtained from the atmosphere while in plants the opposite happens. When these plants are eaten by higher organisms such as humans and animals etc., the glucose can be digested and used right away without further digestion. This is due to the fact that glucose can be absorbed by the blood stream and does not require the help of enzymes or acids to break them down like starches do.

29) Enzymes. As was just explained, enzymes help humans or animals break down (or put together) complex starches into simpler sugars (and vice versa). They are also crucial to digestion and have also been used to cut out parts of DNA so they can be inserted into new organisms. However, enzymes are subject to changes in temperature and PH levels which can reduce their functionality. (See the next chapter for more information.)

30) When cells produce ATP, the conversion to ATP is accompanied by a small loss of energy in the form of heat. The place where this conversion is done is in the mitochondria. Cells that need more energy have more mitochondria to help produce it. This explains why muscle cells have many mitochondria in them. When a person exercises, there is a buildup of metabolic waste in their muscles which makes people feel fatigued. A fresh supply of oxygen is necessary to re-energize their muscles which is why we breathe faster during exercise.

31) When the ATP molecule is "used up" it converts into an ADP molecule. This ADP molecule will be reconverted back to an ATP molecule when a phosphate atom is acquired in the digestion of a complex molecules (e.g. starch) and attached to the existing ADP molecule.

REGENTS REVIEW

1. Some sea slugs store chloroplasts obtained from algae they have ingested. The chloroplasts continue to carry out photosynthesis within the slugs. What advantage would this activity be to these sea slugs?
   (1) The slugs with chloroplasts can synthesize some of their own food.
   (2) The slugs with chloroplasts no longer need to carry out respiration.
   (3) The chloroplasts provide the slugs with camouflage that protects them from UV radiation.
   (4) The chloroplasts contain enzymes that allow the slugs to digest starch.

2. The energy released when sugar molecules are broken down is stored in
   (1) minerals   (3) DNA
   (2) ATP   (4) wastes

A student is opening and closing clothes-pins as part of a lab activity. The student begins to experience muscle fatigue, and the rate at which the student is opening and closing the clothespins slows.

3. The fatigue is due to
   (1) an increase of metabolic waste products in the muscles
   (2) an increase in the pulse rate of the student
   (3) a decrease of metabolic waste products in the muscles
   (4) a decrease in the pulse rate of the student

4. In order for the muscle fatigue to end, the muscle cells must be provided with
   (1) oxygen   (3) carbo dioxide
   (2) nitrogen   (4) amino acids

5. A laboratory technique is represented in the diagram below. Letter A represents a process.

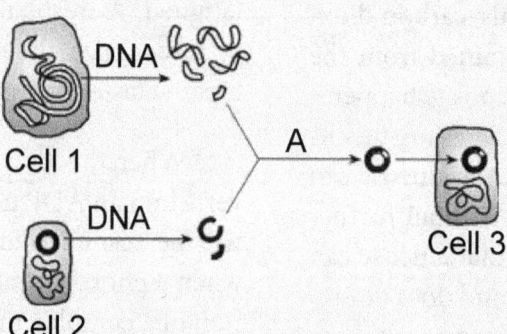

18 | Living Environment Regents Review

Which specific chemicals are needed to success-fully carry out the process shown at A?

(1) receptor molecules
(2) carbohydrates
(3) enzymes
(4) starch molecules

8. During the process of photosynthesis, energy from the Sun is converted into

chemical energy in the bonds of inorganic molecules
chemical energy in the bonds of organic molecules
enzymes used to produce inorganic molecules
enzymes used to produce organic molecules

9. The diagram below represents a cycling of materials.

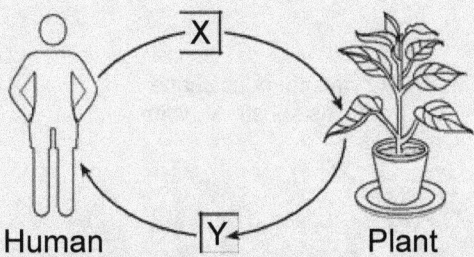

Which row in the chart below shows the substances represented by X and Y?

Row	X	Y
(1)	oxygen	carbon dioxide
(2)	glucose	oxygen
(3)	carbon dioxide	oxygen
(4)	amino acids	carbon dioxide

CHAPTER 5
Enzymes

32) Enzymes are catalysts, something that causes change in another thing. Enzymes are made of proteins that affect another molecule's structure without necessarily undergoing change by itself. Yet, enzymes are affected by their external environment as well. There are 3 factors that shape an enzyme's ability to function.

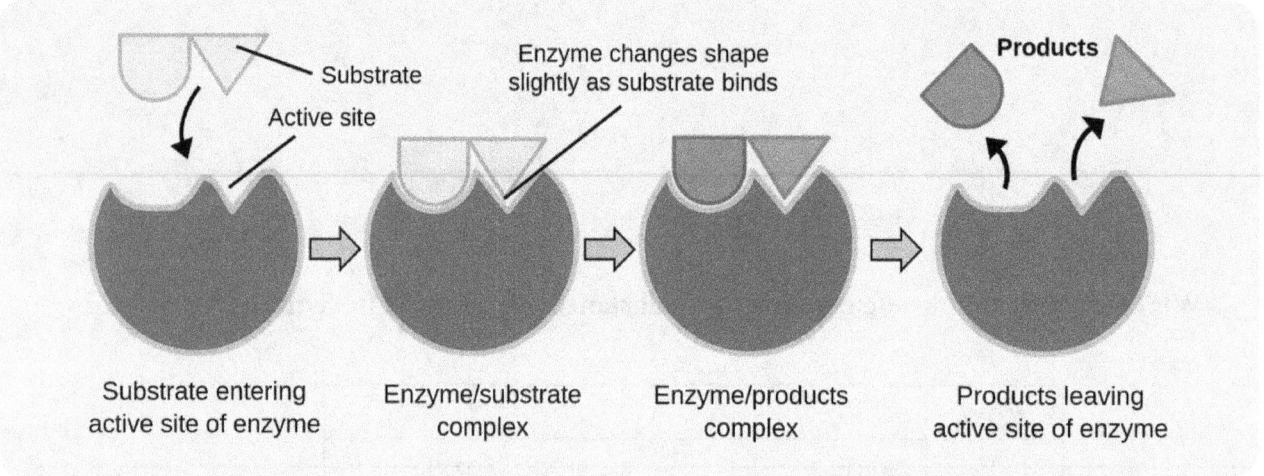

a. **Shape.** If an enzyme's shape is altered for any reason, the enzyme may not be able to catalyze a specific set of molecules and this may disrupt the function of a cell or a group of cells.

b. **Temperature.** The optimal environment in which an enzyme performs in humans is about 98.6°. At higher temperatures, enzyme activity substantially drops as the environment it works in, turns from enzyme-friendly to enzyme-hostile. The enzymes after this point become too fragile to function and they begin to alter their shape temporarily. If the high temperatures are sustained, then the change becomes permanent.

c. **pH levels.** PH levels are the measure of how much acid or base a liquid has. Every liquid has a pH level that ranges between 0-14 with 7 being neutral (tap water has a pH usually between 7-8). The pH levels of *most* bodily fluids are around 7 or 8 and bodily enzymes optimally work at about 7 or 8. When the pH level is altered for whatever reason, it can alter the shape of the enzyme and affect its working ability. In the stomach where the pH levels of the fluids are about 2 or 3, Pepsin, an enzyme found there, works optimally at about 3 pH. In the small intestines where the pH levels are at about 8, the enzyme Trypsin works optimally at about 8 pH.

REGENTS REVIEW

1. Which statement best describes enzymes?

   (1) Every enzyme controls many different reactions.
   (2) The rate of activity of an enzyme might change as pH changes.
   (3) Temperature changes do not affect enzymes.
   (4) Enzymes are produced from the building blocks of carbohydrates.

2. Which statement describes a similarity between all enzymes, antibodies, and hormones?

   (1) Their chemical structure is critical to their ability to function.
   (2) Their ability to replicate identical copies ensures continuation of the species.
   (3) They work better at 100°C than 37°C.
   (4) They are made by and carried by the blood.

3. The diagram below represents a model of a biological process that occurs in humans at normal body temperature, 37°C.

   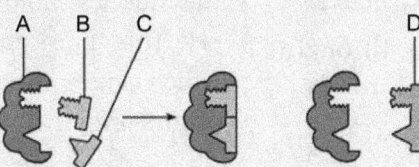

   Increasing body temperature to 40°C would interfere most directly with the rate of function of structure

   (1) A   (3) C
   (2) B   (4) D

4. The graph below shows the results of an action of the enzyme catalase on a piece of meat. Evidence of enzyme activity is indicated by bubbles of oxygen.

   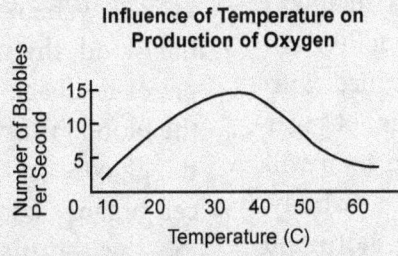

5. Which statement best summarizes the activity of catalase shown in the graph?

   (1) The enzyme works better at 10°C than at 50°C.
   (2) The enzyme works better at 5°C than at 65°C.
   (3) The enzyme works better at 35°C than at either temperature extreme.
   (4) The enzyme works at the same level in all environments.

CHAPTER 6
Homeostasis

Homeostasis

33) Homeostasis means the maintenance of a steady internal environment in face of changing outside conditions. Homeostasis can be observed in organisms in the following ways:

- Some bacteria produce an "antifreeze" when it gets too cold for their existence.
- Many plants close their pores through specialized guard cells in order to preserve water.
- Monarch butterflies migrate when seasons change.
- When we hear a loud noise, our heart rate increases and we become ready for "fight or flight."

34) Dynamic equilibrium. Dynamic equilibrium are small changes that occur all the time in organisms to help them maintain homeostasis. An example of dynamic equilibrium can be seen in the bodies response to a meal with lots of sugars. After the meal, the amount of sugar in the blood, spikes. If left unattended to, it will lead to diabetic shock and then death. The body, in non-diabetics, quickly sends the hormone insulin to rectify that situation by removing the sugar from the blood and bringing it to the cells where the sugar is used.

35) Organisms respond to stimulus through feedback mechanisms. There are two types of feedback: positive feedback and negative feedback.

36) Positive feedback. Positive feedback is a type of feedback (or response) which causes an even greater response in return. In other words, positive feedback creates a cycle of responses until a satisfactory result is attained. An example of this is the birthing process. As the baby pushes to come out (the stimuli) the body sends signals that the muscles should contract to help in the delivery. This then causes to baby to slid even lower which causes even stronger contractions etc. This occurs until the baby is born.

37) Negative feedback. Negative feedback is where an organism responds to a stimulus with a one-time response which takes care of the stimulus. For example, shivering stops the drop in temperature by warming up the body until the body is sufficiently warmed.

38) Feedback works between organs and cells as well. When the glucose level is too high in the blood, the pancreas is prompted (an example of feedback working) to secrete insulin into the blood. This then prompts the cells to absorb the glucose (sugar) in the blood (an example of cell-organ feedback). When the blood level is too low, hormones prompt the opposite reaction. Another example of cell-organ feedback is fast breathing during sports. As one exercises, the cells need more oxygen to maintain the exercise. This prompts faster breathing which gets more oxygen to the cells.

REGENTS REVIEW

The diagram below represents changes in the sizes of openings present in leaves as a result of the actions of cells X and Y.

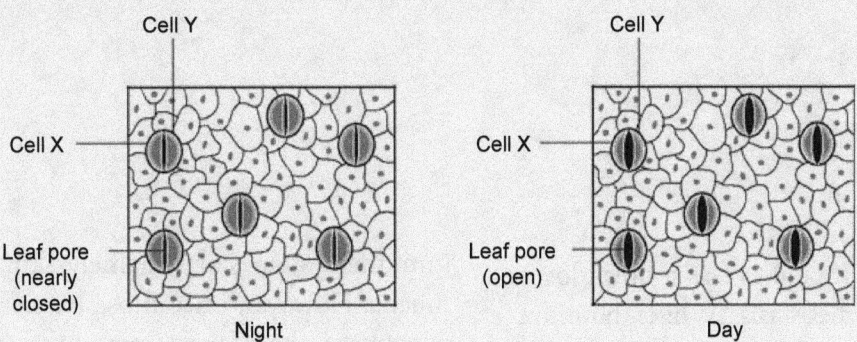

1. The actions of cells X and Y help the plant to
    (1) maintain homeostasis by controlling water loss
    (2) store excess heat during the day and remove the heat at night
    (3) absorb light energy necessary for cellular respiration
    (4) detect changes in the biotic factors present in the environment

2. Breathing rate is constantly being monitored and adjusted in the human body, which results in
    (1) the differentiation of mature body cells
    (2) feedback mechanisms removing damaged cells
    (3) modification of gene activity in cells
    (4) the internal environment being kept within certain limits

3. Homeostasis is maintained in a single-celled organism by the interaction of
    (1) organs   (3) tissues
    (2) systems   (4) organelles

CHAPTER 7
Disease and Homeostasis

39) Disease can be thought of as a breakdown in an organism's homeostasis. While there are many types of diseases, there are two types of diseases which we will discuss here: Pathogens and Cancers.

    a. **Pathogens.** Pathogens include viruses, bacteria, fungi and other parasites which can enter into an organism, overtake the immune system of a person, and harm or kill them.

    b. **Cancer.** Cancer occurs when the genes in a cell which control growth, mutate (don't copy well) and form variant cell parts. These mutated cells can begin to grow uncontrollably and abnormally which results in what is called a tumor. Usually the body detects that there is something wrong in these cells and destroys them. If the body does not destroy them, a life-threatening situation can develop.

The Immune System

40) Humans have many ways in which we protect ourselves against disease before the internal immune system starts, namely skin, saliva, and mucus. However, once those barriers have been penetrated, the internal immune system begins to respond.

- **The immune system** is triggered when the body detects foreign substances floating in it which it does not recognize. It identifies these foreign substances by "reading" the outer layer of each substance in the body. If it detects an unfamiliar molecular pattern on the outside of a substance (called Antigens), it then seeks ways to destroy it through the production of proteins called antibodies. Toxins and poisonous wastes from certain pathogens also can trigger a response from the immune system. In some unfortunate cases, the body mistakenly identifies healthy tissue as an enemy and seeks to destroy it. Examples of this are rheumatoid arthritis (an autoimmune disease), or, when the body rejects a transplant and tries to destroy the transplanted organ. Another example occurs where the body does not recognize insulin and kills it leading to a type of diabetes.

- **White blood cells.** White blood cells play one of the most important roles in the immune system. There are many types of white blood cells and all play a role in killing the invading pathogen. Some surround them or swallow them while others send out antibodies which either kill the invading cell or mark them for death by attaching specified antibodies to the outside of the invader. Most white cells die after doing their job, while others remain and "remember" the way to kill this particular pathogen. The memory can remain for many years, and at a later time, if there is an attack, can reproduce very quickly to fight a new battle.

- **Vaccination.** Vaccination is a system of capturing and killing (or severely weakening) pathogens in a lab and then injecting them into a person's body to "teach" the immune system how to respond to a real future attack. This serum (liquid) is called a vaccine.

- **Damage to the immune system.** Age, stress, and fatigue can all lower the immune system and make a person vulnerable to disease. Some viral diseases such as AIDS kill people by weakening their immune system which then makes them vulnerable even to common infections.

- **Allergies.** Allergies sometimes the body responds to harmless stimuli such as pollen, various foods etc. as an enemy which then causes allergies. While the material that causes the reaction is generally harmless, the reactions the allergies produce may be life threatening. When the body detects allergens, it releases histamines which produces all types of reactions (runny noses, scratchy eyes etc.). People with allergies take anti-histamines to stop the reaction.

REGENTS REVIEW

1. Responses of the immune system to usually harmless environmental substances are known as:
   - (1) antigen production
   - (2) chromosomal mutations
   - (3) pathogens
   - (4) allergies

2. People who have AIDS are more likely than others to become ill with multiple infections because the pathogen that causes AIDS
   - (1) targets many body systems
   - (2) mutates, releasing toxins directly into the bloodstream
   - (3) increases the rate of enzyme activity in different types of body cells
   - (4) damages the immune system

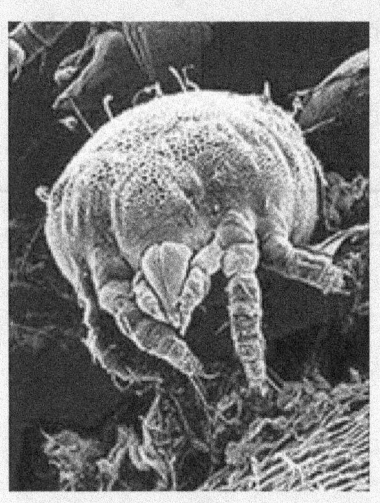

Beware of Dust Mites

Quietly lurking within our mattresses, under our beds, and inside sofas and carpets are creatures too small to be seen with-out a microscope. Dust mites are arthropods closely related to spiders, scorpions, and ticks. They feed on the dead skin cells regularly shed by humans and their animal pets. The average human sheds about 10 grams of dead skin a week. Cats and dogs create even more dander for dust mites to eat. The mites also eat pollen, fungi, and bacteria. They do not drink water but absorb it from the air.

Dust mites do not carry diseases and are harmless to most people. It's their bathroom habits that make some of us itch and sneeze. Many people develop severe allergies to dust mite feces (wastes). If you lie on a rug where dust mites live, you might develop itchy red bumps on your skin. Breathe in dust containing their feces and you might have more serious symptoms, such as difficulty breathing or a severe asthma attack.

Dust mites thrive in warm, humid environments — eating and nesting in dust-collecting bedding, fabric, and carpet. Think about this! A typical mattress can contain anywhere from 100,000 to 10 million dust mites. Nearly 100,000 dust mites can live in one square yard of carpet.

During a process called sensitization, a person's immune system mistakenly identifies the inhaled dust mite waste as an invader. The next time the person is exposed to the dust mite waste, the immune system launches an allergic reaction.

3. **The immune system of an individual who is allergic to dust mite waste produces**
    (1) specialized chemicals that mark dust mite waste for destruction
    (2) viruses that combat dust mites
    (3) white blood cells that attack human skin cells
    (4) white blood cells that attack the skin cells of cats and dog

4. **An allergic reaction occurs when the immune system**
    (1) does not respond to pathogens
    (2) maintains homeostasis
    (3) responds to usually harmless environmental substances
    (4) undergoes rapid, uncontrolled cell division

CHAPTER 8
Reproduction

Reviewed by Rav Chaim Yisroel Belsky Zatza"l

41) Reproduction: there are two types of reproduction: Asexual and Sexual reproduction. Asexual reproduction: the organism reproduces itself and the offspring has the same characteristics (genes) as the parents. Sexual reproduction: both parents join together and produce offspring with some characteristics from each parent.

42) In organisms that reproduce through the second process, the mixing of genes comes from specialized cells which are called Gametes or sex cells.

- **Gametes.** Gametes are cells found both in the male and female. The female produces them in the form of eggs in her ovaries and the male in the form of sperm (seed material) in the testes. These sperm are small egg-shaped cells with tails attached to them which are deposited in the female and meet up with the eggs. These cells are different than regular cells since they only have only one set of genes as opposed to two in regular cells. The reason for having only half of the DNA is so that the two parents' genes can meet up and produce a new being with parts of the male and female genes mixed together.

- **Meiosis.** Meiosis is the process which produces sex cells. The process starts with a cell which has 4 sets of chromosomes. The cell then splits into two different cells each with its own pair of double stranded DNA. The two cells which were created in step one, then break into *4 cells*, each cell containing only **one** chromosome or double strand of DNA. This process creates a sperm cell (in the male) onto which a little tail is attached. In an egg cell (female) the cell breaks up into 4 cells with one large egg cell taking all the cytoplasm (food and nutrients) with it, and leaving 3 small non-functioning cells. (For changes in meiosis and its effects see #50.)

43) Causes of genetic diversity. When two parents combine their genetic code to create offspring, the offspring has a mix of both parents' genes inside. This helps bring about genetic diversity in offspring. Another factor which creates genetic diversity is the result of different splits in Meiosis that occur when the cell (in either the male or female) splits into 4 different cells. Before we begin to explain this process, let's give names to each chromosome. Let's call the 4 chromosomes found in the gamete, chromosome A, B, C, and D. When the cell divides into two, each pair of chromosomes gets a partner. This could lead to A pairing with D or A pairing with B or C etc. Depending on which chromosome lines up with which, will determine the genetic makeup of either the sperm or egg. Furthermore, when the chromosomes line up, genes from say A and D may "go out of line" and crossover to the other side and exchange genes with the other pair of chromosomes. (They never lose "rungs" in the "ladder of DNA" (refer back to # 7 above) they just switch places.) Thus, by going out of line, and switching places on the DNA, the DNA gets shuffled which further contributes to genetic diversity.

44) During fertilization, the gametes come together, and a new cell called a zygote is formed which contains all the information needed by the offspring for its future life. This process is called recombination. This zygote will then split into 4 and then start to differentiate (in a process called differentiation) which eventually will lead to the formation of organs by the process of Mitosis. (Mitosis is the process in which a cell divides and makes a new and exact copy of the original cell, complete with all its chromosomes. Mitosis occurs not only at birth but all the time, in every cell type in the body. This occurs due to the fact that old cells are always dying off and new cells are being born.) The cells then form an embryo which is an organism at an early stage of development.

45) In the first few months of a baby's development, many of the baby's essential organs develop. They develop inside an amniotic sack and use the Placenta to provide food and oxygen from the mother's blood while removing wastes from the baby in exchange. After the first few months pass, the baby is now a developed fetus. During the first few months, many things can go wrong in the development of a baby. The environment plays an important role in the development of the fetus and in the potential for problems. For ex. smoking, consumption of alcohol and other environmental hazards can harm the development of the fetus. Therefore, it is important during this early stage, that pregnant women take heed not to expose themselves to toxins or alcohol which can damage the early development of crucial organs.

46) Hormones play an important role in both males and females during reproduction. Estrogen and Progesterone play an important role in female reproductive development, while Testosterone plays an important part in a male's reproductive development.

- With the knowledge of how reproduction works, scientists have greatly increased the chances and abilities for people to have children. Examples of such techniques are In-vitro fertilization and Hormone therapy. These techniques and therapies have enabled people who have difficulty conceiving to do so where it was difficult or almost impossible in the past.

- Cloning. Cloning is a process where scientists remove the "half set" of DNA (genes) from the egg of the female and then insert in its nucleus a full set of DNA from the females cells. If this egg then reproduces, its offspring will have exactly the same genes as its parent.

REGENTS REVIEW

1. Which factor has the greatest influence on the development of new, inheritable characteristics?

    (1) combinations of genes resulting from mitosis
    (2) mutations of genes in reproductive cells
    (3) sorting of genes during asexual reproduction
    (4) recombining of genes during differentiation

2. Which process allows a mammal to continue to grow in size?

    (1) mitosis of sex cells
    (2) mitosis of body cells
    (3) meiosis of sex cells
    (4) meiosis of body cells

3. An organism that reproduces asexually will have offspring that have

    (1) the same genetic information as both of its parents
    (2) different genetic information from either of its parents
    (3) the same genes as its parent
    (4) different genes from its parent

4. Scientists have found a gene in the DNA of a certain plant that could be the key to increasing the amount of lycopene, a cancer-fighting substance, in tomatoes.

    The ability to produce increased amounts of lycopene will be passed on to new tomato cells as a direct result of

    (1) recycling
    (2) mitosis
    (3) enzyme action
    (4) gene expression

The diagram below represents some stages that occur in the formation of an embryo.

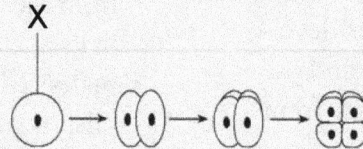

5. Which statement best describes stage X?

    (1) Stage X is a zygote and contains half the number of chromosomes as the body cells of the parents.
    (2) Stage X is formed by the process of meiosis and is known as a gamete.
    (3) Stage X is a zygote and is formed as a result of the process of fertilization.
    (4) Stage X is formed by mitosis and is known as an egg cell.

6. Modern technology could be used to clone pet dogs and cats. The cloned animals would resemble the original pets because

   (1) the genes of the new animals are different from those of the original pets
   (2) half of the genetic information of the new animals is the same as that of the original pets
   (3) the new animals have mutations not found in the original pets
   (4) the new animals have the same genetic information as the original pets

7. Which situation would be part of the normal reproductive cycle of a human?

   the presence of testosterone regulating gamete production in a male
   estrogen in concentrations that would produce sperm in a female
   a high progesterone level in a male
   a low insulin level in either a male or a female

8. Which organism would most likely have new gene combinations?

   (1) a frog that was produced from a skin cell of a frog
   (2) a hamster resulting from sexual reproduction
   (3) a bacterium resulting from asexual reproduction
   (4) a starfish that grew from part of a starfish

9. A scientist claimed that he had cloned a guinea pig to produce two offspring, a male and a female. The claim is not valid because

   (1) guinea pigs can reproduce both sexually and asexually
   (2) the two offspring are not identical copies of the original guinea pig
   (3) each of the offspring had half the genetic information of the original guinea pig
   (4) none of the genetic information came from the original guinea pig

10. The major function of the placenta is to
    (1) cushion the fetus so it won't be hurt when the mother moves
    (2) exchange food, oxygen, and waste between mother and fetus
    (3) store food for the fetus
    (4) support the egg for the process of fertilization

Base your answers to question 11 on the diagram below and on your knowledge of biology. The diagram represents the reproductive cycle of a squirrel species with 40 chromosomes in each zygote.

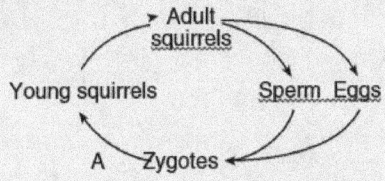

11. A process that could be represented by A is
    (1) fertilization
    (2) meiosis
    (3) mitosis
    (4) mutation

12. Some goats have been genetically modified with a human gene that codes for a blood anticlotting factor. The anticlotting factor can then be extracted from the goat milk and used during surgery. To produce these genetically modified goats, scientists most likely
    (1) injected the anticlotting factor into the milk-producing glands of the animals
    (2) added modified DNA into the milk of the animals
    (3) inserted the human gene into the egg cells of goats
    (4) altered the nutritional requirements of newborn goats

13. Which statement describes a function of the human male reproductive system?
    (1) It produces gametes in testes.
    (2) It supplies a fluid that protects the fetus.
    (3) It provides support for the development of the embryo.
    (4) It provides nutrient materials through a placenta

14. Exposure to toxins during early stages of pregnancy is more likely to cause birth defects than exposure in late pregnancy because
    (1) essential organs form during early development
    (2) the uterus provides more protection in late pregnancy
    (3) the placenta forms during late pregnancy
    (4) meiosis occurs rapidly during early development

15. Although a liver cell and a muscle cell in a human developed from the same single cell, their appearance and functions are different. This is because the liver cell
    (1) contains different genes than the muscle cell
    (2) expresses different genes than the muscle cell
    (3) destroys the muscle cell genes it contains
    (4) lacks the genes found in muscle cells

16. Sexual reproduction in a species usually results in
    (1) an increase in the chromosome number in the offspring
    (2) offspring genetically identical to the parent
    (3) recombination of genes
    (4) a decrease in biodiversity

Two methods of reproduction are represented in the diagram below.

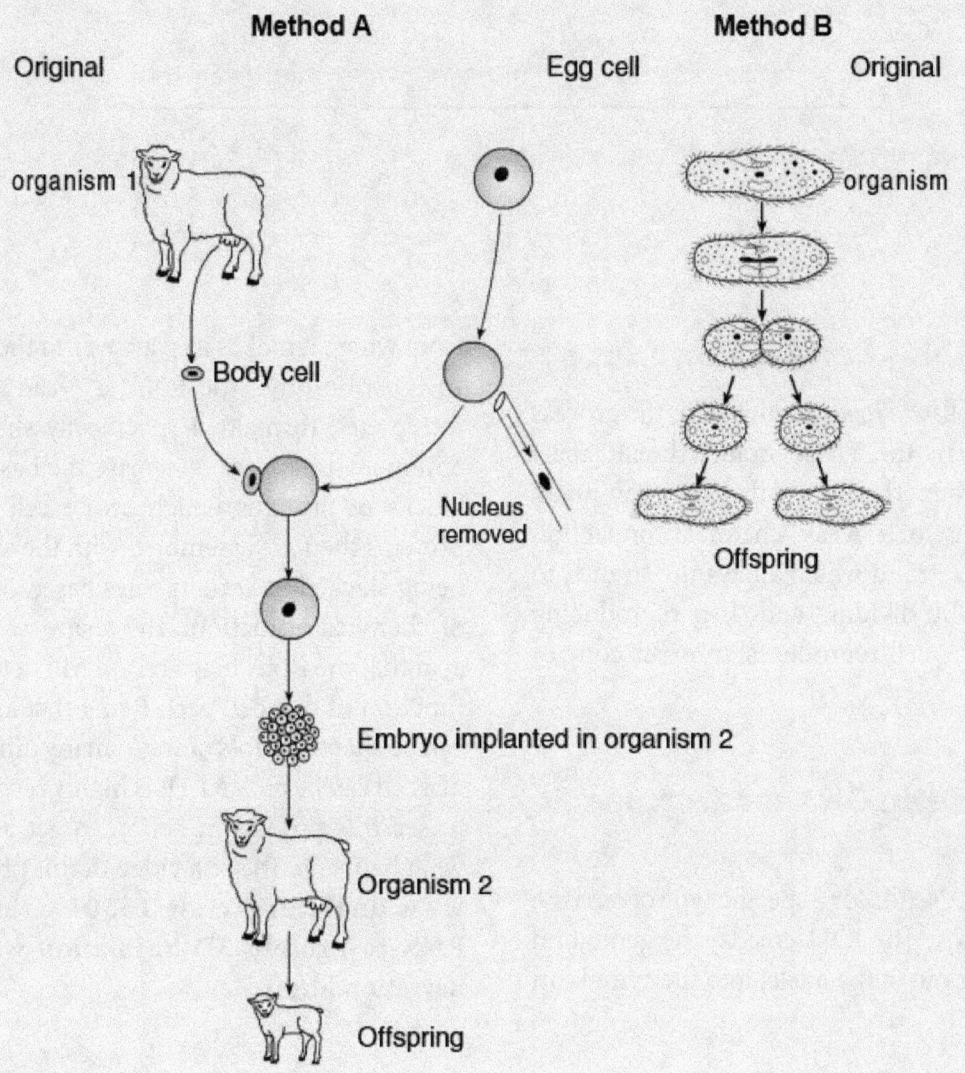

17. How does the DNA in the offspring produced by these methods compare to the DNA in the original organism?

   (1) The offspring contain half the original number of chromosomes in each method.
   (2) The DNA in the offspring is genetically identical to that of the original organism in both methods.
   (3) The offspring produced by method A contain twice the original number of genes, while those produced by method B contain half the original number of genes.
   (4) The number of DNA bases is less than that of the original organism in method A, but more than the original number in method B.

CHAPTER 9
DNA Action and Replication

What enables cells to reproduce?

47) When cells are ready to divide (in the process called mitosis), the DNA strands break apart from each other. The reason that they can break apart is because of a "weak" chemical connection between each strand which allows the strands to break apart. By dividing and then reproducing new DNA, the cell reproduces an exact copy of itself.

How does the DNA create specific cell parts?

48) The DNA sends for a specific type of enzyme known as RNA. The RNA "reads" the genes and then transfers out of the nuclei into the cytoplasm from where it makes its way over to the ribosome. In the ribosome, the RNA is "read" and again interpreted to make a specifically shaped set of amino acids. Amino acids are the basic building blocks of proteins which create cell parts. The proteins then are assembled with the amino acids being stacked in certain ways based on the areas of chemical attraction. The shape of the amino acid that the RNA helps create will determine the function of that cell part. Being that amino acids can be shaped in lots of ways; many different parts of a cell can be created. (It is highly recommended to see this process in action to get a picture of what happens. To see a video of this process go to www.dnalc.org/view/15501-Translation-RNA-to-protein-3D-animation-with-basic-narration.html)

REGENTS REVIEW

The process represented in the diagram below occurs in many cells.

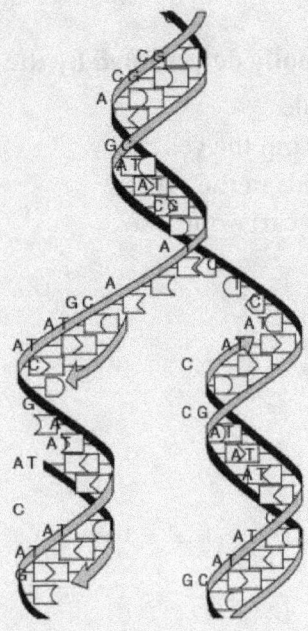

1. The main function of this process is to:
   (1) provide an exact copy of the genetic code
   (2) ensure genetic variation in a species
   (3) synthesize cellular proteins
   (4) produce antibodies to combat disease

2. The way a protein molecule is folded determines the shape of the molecule, which determines the
   (1) function of that protein
   (2) structure of ATP containing that protein
   (3) type of simple sugars in that protein
   (4) amino acids in that protein

3. Changing one base in a gene could have the most direct effect on the
   (1) function of the membrane of a cell
   (2) sequence of building blocks of a protein found in a cell
   (3) number of mitochondria in a cell
   (4) type of carbohydrates synthesized by a cell

4. A pesticide that kills an insect by interfering with the production of proteins in the insect would most directly affect the activity of
   (1) Ribosomes
   (2) Minerals
   (3) chloroplasts
   (4) mitochondria

5. The shape of a protein is originally determined by the
   (1) size of the protein molecule
   (2) location of the protein within the cell
   (3) arrangement of amino acids in the protein
   (4) function the protein must carry out

CHAPTER 10
Mutations and Individuality

Heredity

49) Heredity is the study of the passage of certain genes from generation to generation. The one who uncovered the basic rules governing heredity was a monk by the name of Gregory Mendel who discovered the concept of dominant and passive traits[1] in his work on peas.

Mutations

50) Any change in the DNA is called a mutation. If a different base of the DNA is created (or inserted or deleted) at the time that the cells undergo mitosis, a different amino acid will be created later on. If a gene is skipped or added, the resulting genes which come after it will also be altered (like skipping a question on your answer key during a test). Many times, the cause of these mutations is due to some outside force such as exposure to some chemical or radiation in the environment. However, these mutations will affect that person and not produce changes that will be passed down to the next generation. For a mutation to be passed on to the next generation, *the mutations must occur in the sex cells (either egg or sperm) and then be passed down to the next generation.*

If a mutation does not cause the cell to die, **and** happens in the sex cells, it can be passed down to the organism's offspring. This can result in what's called a hereditary disease. The result of a mutation in the sex cells can cause Down Syndrome (not thought to be a hereditary disease) and Sickle Cell Anemia (hereditary) where the structure of the amino acids are altered and where sickle shaped blood cells occur impeding normal living conditions.

Individual Cells

51) If all the cells of a person contain a person's entire DNA, why is it that there is such diversity in the body? The reason for this is because all cells only use selective parts of their DNA when shaping a cell part. What influences which parts of the DNA will be turned on? Either internal or external factors. An example of an internal factor is a hormone which can turn on specific genes. Alternatively, an organism's environment can either repress or express a certain gene. Thus, identical twins, although they have identical genes, can be very different from each other because of their different environments. When certain genes are activated they are called expressed genes; when they are inactive they are called repressed genes.

REGENTS REVIEW

1. In the summer, the arctic fox appears brown because its cells produce a dark pigment. However, in the winter, the arctic fox appears white because the dark pigment is not produced. The color change is most likely due to the effect of

    (1) different genes produced in the different seasons
    (2) increased pollution on genetic mutations
    (3) environmental conditions on gene expression
    (4) poor nutrition on cell growth and development

2. Many years ago, a scientist grew pea plants that produced wrinkled peas. The peas from these plants produced new plants that also produced wrinkled peas. The scientist concluded that something in the parent plants was being transmitted to the next generation. This discovery is now known as

    (1) genetic engineering
    (2) biological evolution
    (3) heredity
    (4) natural selection

3. Which statement concerning cell communication is correct?

    (1) DNA codes for certain molecules that become cell receptors involved in cell communication.
    (2) Cells produce ATP molecules, which become cell receptors for communication.
    (3) Cells build new cell parts, which function as communication genes.
    (4) Certain proteins use cell communication to build new cell parts made of DNA.

4. A towel placed on a lawn for a length of time can cause the grass beneath it to lose its green color. The most probable explanation for this is that darkness

    (1) affects the expression of certain genes in the grass
    (2) causes a mutation in the plants
    (3) affects the structure of cell membranes in the grass
    (4) causes plants to switch to heterotrophic nutrition

The diagram below represents one process that might occur in cells.

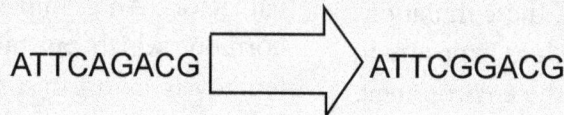

5. Which process is represented in the diagram?

    (1) cell reproduction
    (2) meiosis
    (3) mutation
    (4) gene replication

An alteration of genetic information is shown below.

A-G-T-A-C-C-G-A-T → A-G-T-G-A-T

6. This type of alteration of the genetic information is an example of
   (1) deletion
   (2) insertion
   (3) substitution
   (4) recombination

The diagram below represents genetic material.

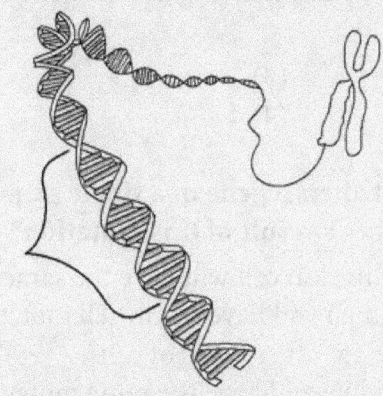

7. The expression of the section labeled X may be modified by
   (1) temperature, only
   (2) asexual reproduction
   (3) the environment
   (4) pH, only

8. Which situation results in a characteristic that is inheritable?
   (1) A limb is lost when two marine organisms fight.
   (2) A puppy learns to beg for food by watching an older dog perform tricks.
   (3) A gene is inserted into a bacterium, allowing the organism to produce insulin.
   (4) A random mutation causes the immediate death of a microbe.

A sample of body cells and samples of sex cells received from four members of a species are screened for the presence of a specific gene mutation. The results of the gene-testing procedure conducted on the cells are shown in the table below.

Species Member Tested	Type of Cells Tested and the Result (+ = mutation present, - = mutation absent)		
	Body Cells	Sperm	Egg
1	+		+
2	+	+	
3	-		+
4	+	-	

9. Which species member would be unlikely to pass the gene mutation on to its offspring?

   (1) 1
   (2) 2
   (3) 3
   (4) 4

10. A deletion of a DNA segment alters a gene in a single skin cell of an individual. Which statement best describes a result of this mutation?

    (1) Any cell produced from this skin cell will have the same mutation.
    (2) All offspring of the individual will have a skin cell mutation.
    (3) The mutation will spread into other types of cells.
    (4) The gametes of this individual will have the same mutation.

11. Some bacteria are unable to survive unless a certain nutrient is present in their food supply. After exposure to ultraviolet radiation, some of these bacteria are able to synthesize this nutrient. This change is most likely due to

    (1) increased respiration
    (2) exposure to an antigen
    (3) an alteration in a gene
    (4) gamete formation

CHAPTER 11
Genetic Engineering and Biotechnology

Selective Breeding

52) Selective breeding is an ancient practice in which two organisms, which exhibit certain traits, are paired together to produce a certain strain of an organism or a high-quality line of that organism.

Genetic Engeneering

53) Using their knowledge of science, scientists have been able to manipulate organism's genes to be better equipped to survive and fight certain diseases. For example, scientists have put genes into certain plants that produce chemicals to kill off insects that eat them up. The way the gene is placed into the new plant is through a method like "cut and paste" in word processing programs. This process uses certain enzymes which splice a part of a gene out of resistant organism's DNA and then splice it into the plant that wants the resistance to it. Another application of this technology is where DNA is put into bacteria and induced to produce a certain hormone such as insulin. A third application is where DNA is used to fight crime. The DNA sample from a crime scene is copied over many times until forensic detectives can use it to figure out who committed a crime.

Applications of Biotechnology

54) The applications of biotechnology are many and growing. Scientists study the Genome (all the genes in an organism) and are constantly figuring out what genes turn on which diseases. Additionally, scientists have begun to discover how to alter DNA to cure diseases or help people who can't produce a certain hormone, to do so. Unfortunately, by placing DNA in bacteria, while the desired effect is achieved, harmful side effects from the bacteria can make the DNA unsafe to use. In the future, synthetic DNA may provide the relief people are seeking.

REGENTS REVIEW

1. The Old English Bulldog is extinct. To produce a new English Bulldog, dogs having the desired physical features, but not the aggressive nature of the old bulldogs, were mated. The result was a bulldog that was similar in appearance to the extinct bulldog, but without its fierce nature. Which technique was most likely used to develop this new variety of dog?
    (1) cloning
    (2) inducing mutations
    (3) genetic engineering
    (4) selective breeding

2. For those individuals who have an allergic reaction to cats, a company in Los Angeles promises relief. They offer a new line of cats genetically modified to eliminate or reduce their allergy-causing properties. The development of this new line of cats most likely involved
    (1) using natural selection to produce a new variety of cat
    (2) altering the reproductive rate of cats
    (3) changing the behavior of cats
    (4) manipulating the DNA of cats

3. Scientists have found a gene in the DNA of a certain plant that could be the key to increasing the amount of lycopene, a cancer-fighting substance, in tomatoes. The process of inserting this gene into the DNA of a tomato plant is known as
    (1) selective breeding   (3) cloning
    (2) genetic engeneering   (4) replication

4. Domestic horses have a greater diversity of coat colors than that of wild horses. The process that led to a greater diversity of coat colors in domestic horses is
    (1) selective breeding   (3) gene alteration
    (2) random mutation   (4) natural selection

5. Selective breeding has been used for thousands of years to
    (1) develop bacteria that produce human insulin
    (2) clone desirable plant varieties
    (3) develop viruses that protect against diseases
    (4) produce new varieties of domestic animals

CHAPTER 12
Ecology

55) Life on earth is interdependent and living things rely on outside factors and others to survive. All the living things which interact with each other, make up an ecosystem. For example: all the plants, bacteria and animals that interact with each other make up an ecosystem. Thus, an Ecosystem is a portion of the environment and all the interactions that happen in it. Each piece of living matter in an ecosystem is called a biotic factor.

56) When studying an ecosystem, scientists also study non-living matter, such as soil, water etc., and how they impact living matter. That non-living material is called abiotic matter. For example: a fish in a pond interacts with biotic matter- other fish, (eating them), and abiotic matter (with water).

57) While an organism can potentially live in a number of places, it usually finds itself in one place called a habitat. An ocean, pond, lake, or desert are all examples of habitats.

58) All the organisms that live in a specific area are called a population. For example- all the termites living on one termite mound make up the termite's population. All the combined population's living in a habitat are called a community. All the organisms on Earth combine to make the earth's biosphere. Any place where life exits is part of Earth's biosphere.

59) Every ecosystem is dependent on the amount of resources that community can extract from the environment. Because resources are finite, struggle becomes an essential part of living. This struggle is called competition. Competition keeps the number of species in check by limiting growth.

Examples of abiotic and biotic factors which limit the growth of a species:

60) Abiotic factors:
oxygen: if there is not enough oxygen in water, some species of fish will not be able to live there. Sunlight: sunlight filtering to the bottom of a forest floor will also limit what types of plants can inhabit the forest floor. Climate: only some species can survive in certain climates.

61) Biotic factors: predators: limit the size of a population by eating up their prey. If too many prey are killed, this limits the size of a *predator's* population being that their resources become sparse. This then begins a reverse cycle where the prey begins to flourish until the next cycle begins. The number of organisms that an ecosystem can carry is called the ecosystem's carrying capacity. The number of organisms increase in a habitat until they reach carrying capacity, based on both biotic and abiotic factors, and then level off.

REGENTS REVIEW

1. A scientist was studying a population of fish in a pond over a period of 10 years. He observed that the population increased each year for 3 years, and then remained nearly constant for the rest of the study. The best explanation for this observation is that the population had
    (1) stopped reproducing
    (2) reached carrying capacity
    (3) mutated into a different species
    (4) run out of food and migrated to a different pond

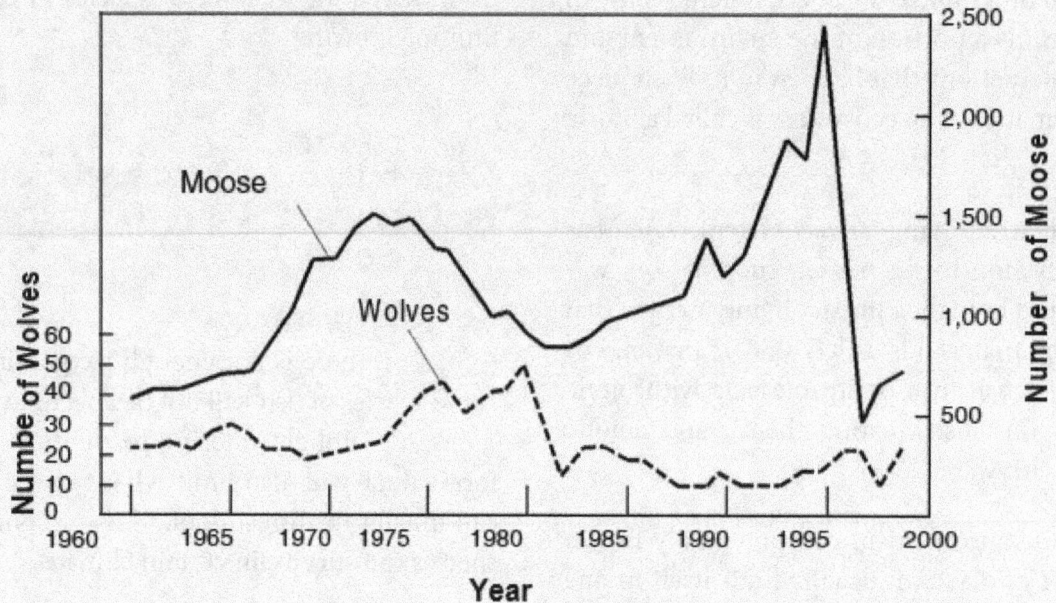

Wolf and Moose Populations on Isle Royale, 1960 to 1999

2. What is the relationship between a wolf and a moose?
    (1) wolf - prey; moose - predator
    (2) wolf - parasite; moose - host
    (3) wolf - predator; moose - decomposer
    (4) wolf - predator; moose - prey

3. State one possible reason for the change in the moose population between 1995 and 1997.

4. In order for an ecosystem to remain stable there must be
    (1) drastic modifications to the environment
    (2) interrelationships and interdependencies among organisms
    (3) limited biodiversity
    (4) gradual changes in the climate

5. The chart below shows three ecological terms used to describe levels of organization on Earth.

A	ecosystem
B	population
C	biosphere

Which diagram best represents the relationship of these ecological terms?

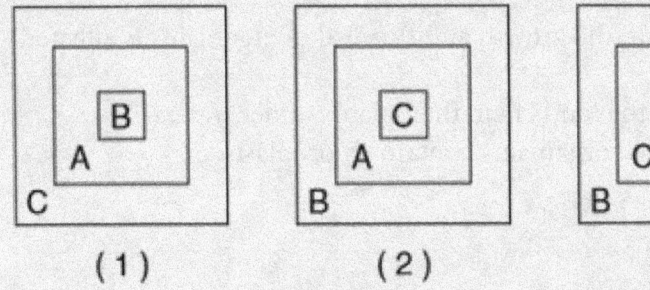
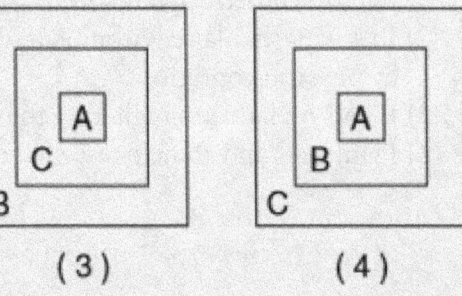

6. Which characteristic of a geographic region would have the greatest influence on the type of ecosystem that forms in that region?
    (1) ratio of autotrophs to heterotrophs
    (2) concentration of atmospheric oxygen
    (3) number of food chains
    (4) climatic conditions

7. Plants are green because they contain the protein chlorophyll. A bucket was left on the lawn for one week. When the bucket was removed, the grass under the bucket had turned from green to a yellowish white color. This change is due to the interaction between the grass and
    (1) decomposer organisms in the soil, an abiotic factor
    (2) the amount of sunlight, an abiotic factor
    (3) increased moisture under the bucket, a biotic factor
    (4) the metal composition of the bucket, a biotic factor

8. Which statement best explains why different plant species are found at different water depths as represented in the diagram below?

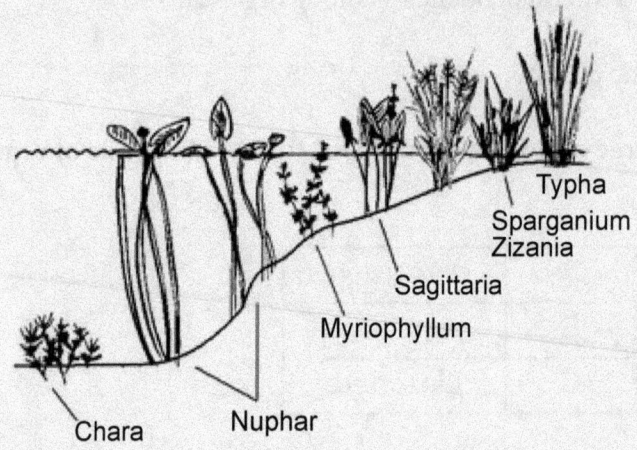

(1) Energy flows through ecosystems in one direction, typically beginning with photo-synthetic organisms.
(2) In any particular environment, the growth and survival of organisms is affected by physical conditions.
(3) Plants on land are higher up the food chain than plants under water.
(4) Plant cells and some one-celled organisms contain chloroplasts.

CHAPTER 13
Relationships in Ecosystems

62) Many types of living matter depend on other living things to survive. For example: termites use a one celled organism to digest food, without which it would not be able to survive. Another example occurs when sharks eat their prey the smaller fish below the shark eat up the scraps of half eaten fish that drift down underneath.

63) Food Chains-animals are part of food chains. This chain occurs as larger animals eat up smaller animals (part of a predator-prey relationship).

Two types of energy acquisition

63) There are two ways in which organisms acquire energy. Some organism are autotrophs-producers in which they self-produce their own food, For example Algae derives its energy from the sun. Another type of organism is known as a heterotroph-consumers. These organisms acquire energy by eating food outside themselves. Among heterotrophs there are two different types: herbivores- animals that acquire their food by consuming plants and carnivores-animals that acquire their energy needs through the consumption of other animals. Omnivore-animals that eat both plants and animals for their energy.

64) When animals die, other organisms eat their bodies. These organisms who digest dead organisms are known as decomposers. Fungi, and other bacteria sometimes do this.

65) There are some carnivores like vultures that don't kill their prey rather they eat off dead carcasses. They are called scavengers. There are some organisms called parasites which live off a host's body. They usually don't kill their hosts, although at times they do. Scientists also divide species into two types-producers and consumers. Producers make/provide the goods while consumers use it (or eat it up).

66) Scientists use a model called a food web or food chain to show the relationships between predator/prey or parasite/hosts etc. Every animal and species fits into an ecological niche (place) of its own.

REGENTS REVIEW

1. Four levels of an energy pyramid are represented below.

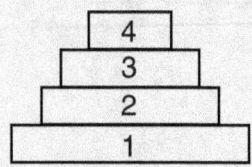

   Which statement about this energy pyramid is correct?
   (1) Organisms in level 4 receive their energy directly from the Sun
   (2) Organisms in level 2 are carnivores
   (3) Organisms in level 2 receive their energy from level 3
   (4) Organisms in level 1 are autotrophic

2. A certain fungus can be harmful when it infects the outermost layers of the human foot, while another type of fungus can be beneficial when it recycles nutrients by breaking down dead organisms. Which terms identify these two roles of fungi?
   (1) producer, prey
   (2) host, autotroph
   (3) parasite, decomposer
   (4) herbivore, predator

The diagram below represents a food web composed of producers, consumers, and decomposers.

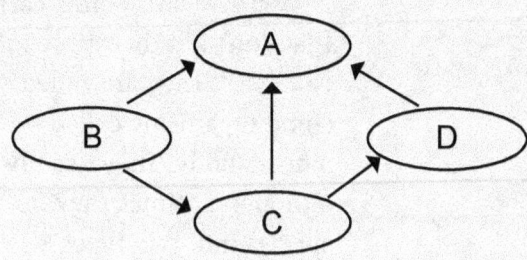

3. Which group would represent the decomposer organisms?
   (1) A   (3) C
   (2) B   (4) D

Keystone Species

A keystone species is one whose presence contributes to the diversity of life and whose extinction would lead to the extinction of other forms of life. A keystone species helps to support the ecosystem of which it is a part.

An example of what can happen when a keystone species is removed occurred when fur hunters eliminated sea otters from some Pacific Ocean kelp beds. Otters eat sea urchins, which eat kelp. With its major predator gone, sea urchin populations exploded and consumed most of the kelp. Fish, snails, and other animals associated with the kelp beds disappeared.

The grizzly bear is another example of a keystone species. Grizzlies transfer nutrients from the ocean ecosystem to the forest ecosystem. The first stage of this transfer is performed by salmon that swim up rivers, sometimes for hundreds of miles. Salmon are rich in nitrogen, sulfur, carbon, and phosphorus. The bears capture the salmon and carry them onto dry land, scattering nutrient-rich feces (wastes) and partially eaten salmon carcasses. It has been estimated that the bears leave up to half of the salmon they harvest on the forest floor.

Questions 4-6

4. One action humans can take that might ensure that these sea otters will continue their function as a keystone species in their environment is to
    (1) establish a sea otter wildlife refuge in the Atlantic Ocean
    (2) pass laws to regulate the hunting of sea otters
    (3) plant kelp in the Pacific Ocean
    (4) destroy sea urchins found living in the kelp beds

5. Which organism is most likely not functioning as a keystone species in its ecosystem?
    (1) beaver — transforms its territory from a stream to a pond or swamp, maintaining the habitat for a variety of native species
    (2) elephant — destroys trees, making room for grass species and preventing the environment from becoming a woodland
    (3) black-tailed prairie dogs — burrows act as homes to other creatures, including burrowing owls, badgers, rabbits, snakes, salamanders, and insects
    (4) zebra mussels — compete with native species, reducing the biodiversity of the Great Lakes ecosystem

6. Which sequence best represents the feeding relationships in a kelp ecosystem that has not been disturbed by humans?
    (1) sea urchins → kelp → fish
    (2) kelp → sea urchins → sea otters
    (3) kelp → sea otters → sea urchins
    (4) sea urchins → snails → kelp

The diagram below represents interactions between organisms in a stable ecosystem.

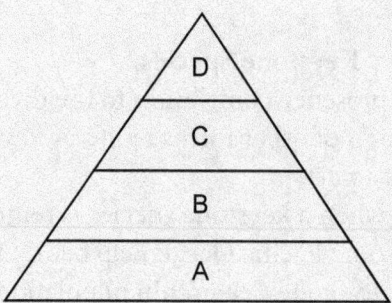

7. **Which statement correctly describes organisms in this ecosystem?**
    (1) Organisms in level B obtain their energy directly from the Sun.
    (2) Organisms in level C obtain their nutrients directly from organisms in level D.
    (3) Organisms in level A are herbivores.
    (4) Organisms in level D are heterotrophic

8. **Which statement best describes bat populations in a stable ecosystem?**
    (1) They are held in check by environmental factors.
    (2) They are producers that rely indirectly on other producers.
    (3) They are not limited by natural predators.
    (4) They are not dependent on other species

9. **When two different bird species temporarily occupy the same niche, they would most likely**
    (1) change their nesting behaviors
    (2) not affect one another
    (3) interbreed to form a new species
    (4) compete with one another

10. **Which group would most likely be represented in a food chain?**
    (1) biotic factors
    (2) abiotic factors
    (3) inorganic compounds
    (4) finite resources

11. **Which statement describes an activity of a decomposer?**
    (1) A mushroom digests and absorbs nutrients from organic matter.
    (2) A sunflower uses nutrients from the soil to make proteins.
    (3) A snail scrapes algae off rocks in an aquarium.
    (4) A hawk eats and digests a mouse.

12. **A relationship between a consumer and producer is best illustrated by a**
    (1) snake eating a bird
    (2) tree absorbing minerals
    (3) fungus breaking down wastes
    (4) deer eating grass

13. Which statement represents a characteristic of an ecosystem that is not likely to sustain itself?
    (1) The Sun provides the needed energy.
    (2) Energy is transferred from plants to animals.
    (3) There are more consumers than producers.
    (4) There are interactions between biotic and abiotic factors.

Euglena are single-celled organisms that live in ponds. All euglena have chloroplasts and can make their own food. They can also take in food from the environment. The diagram below represents a euglena.

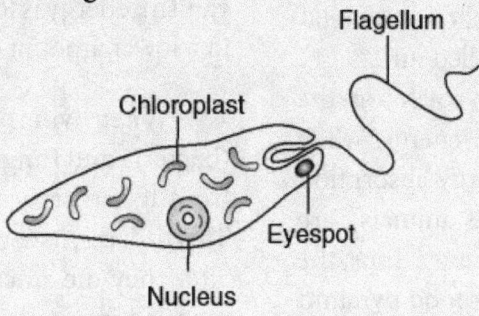

14. Euglena can be classified as both
    (1) an autotroph and a parasite
    (2) a decomposer and a heterotroph
    (3) a producer and a parasite
    (4) an autotroph and a heterotroph

15. Puppies are often given medicine to eliminate roundworms from their intestines. These worms consume some of the food the puppies have digested. The worms and the puppies represent a relationship known as
    (1) predator - prey
    (2) consumer - producer
    (3) parasite - host
    (4) autotroph - heterotroph

Grasses → Elk → Wolves

Wolves in the park were killed or driven off by humans in the 1920s and 1930s. In the winter of 1995, humans released 17 wolves from Canada into the park. A year later, 14 more wolves were released.

16. One possible reason that the wolves were released into the park was to
    (1) eliminate unwanted autotrophs
    (2) reduce an overpopulation of elk
    (3) provide food for small predators
    (4) increase the number of herbivores

17. After the wolves were released, the populations of some scavengers increased. This was most likely due to
    (1) a reduction in predator populations
    (2) a decrease in the number of grasses
    (3) an increase in the number of dead elk
    (4) an increase in water supplies

CHAPTER 14
Energy Recycling

68) Energy pyramid: being that the sun is the primary source of energy for the world, scientists created a diagram which shows the relationship of animals to the sun called an energy pyramid. Organisms which rely solely on the sun are shown to have the most energy, while the ones with the least direct energy absorption from the sun (such as carnivorous animals), are shown with the least amount of energy. Thus, the animals that are at the top of their food pyramid many times receive the least (stored up) energy. The reason for this is due to the fact that as one organism consumes and processes another organism, energy is lost in the form of heat resulting in a lower amount of stored energy.

69) When living organisms die off, decomposers (bacteria and fungi) strip every last bit of energy from it and return the energy back to the soil. This process, in a way, keeps organisms alive even after they die since the organism now becomes recycled into nutrients in the soil which end up later in animals' bodies (when the animals eat the plants) and then into humans (when humans eat animals).

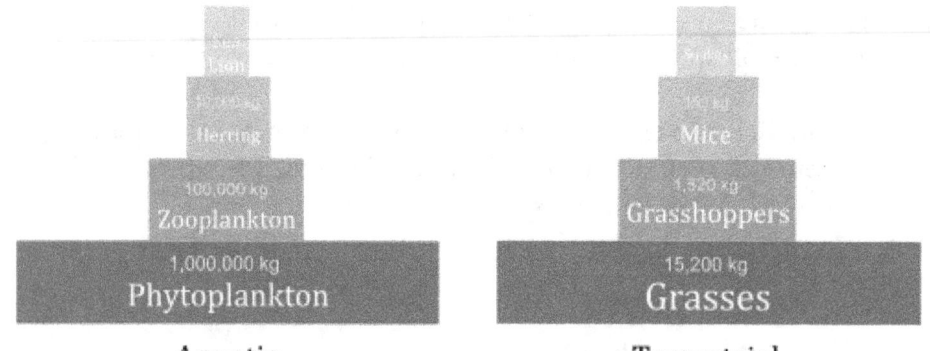

By Swiggity.Swag.YOLO.Bro - Own work, CC BY-SA 4.0, https://commons.wikimedia.org/w/index.php?curid=40717527

REGENTS REVIEW

1. Which term refers to the ecological niche of many bacteria and fungi in an ecosystem?
    (1) decomposer
    (2) herbivore
    (3) producer
    (4) scavenger

CHAPTER 15
Biodiversity and Environmental changes

70) Life benefits from having many types of different species. This concept is called **Biodiversity**. There are three principal benefits to biodiversity.

a. If there is a disease in an ecosystem, not all the organisms will perish since some may be immune to it. For ex. if a disease strikes a farm with many types of crops in it, being that there are many species which are not affected by this particular disease, these crops act as a natural barrier to the spread of the disease. In contrast, if a disease strikes a farm with a single crop, then if the disease hurts the crop, the whole farm may die out.

b. A loss of biodiversity leads in many cases to a loss of stability in the whole ecosystem since all life exists interdependently. Thus, large scale clearings of rain forests can upset a whole ecosystem and all its interdependent variables. Another example occurs after natural pesky predators are eliminated and the hunted prey experience a boom in that particular population. This boom, while seemingly positive, down the line may lead to mass starvation (among the prey) as an increase of competition occurs.

c. Finally, if biodiversity is lost, we (potentially) lose valuable genetic resources which could have helped humans find cures for diseases etc.

71) As natural changes occur in the environment, life and the accompanying ecosystem change with it as well. This change is referred to as **ecological succession**. As the old environment changes, the previous ecosystem may find itself fighting to survive and die out. For example, as mosses grow they provide a deep organic root which can offer a place for shrubs to sink their roots into. When the shrubs grow, they may block out the sunlight that allowed the grasses to grow (that gave them their place) and the mosses may die out.

72) There are two common examples of ecological succession. One, where an environment changes from a bare rocky place to a fertile forest over time. Another common example can be found where a lake changes to a forest as the lake dries up and provides a fertile place for trees to take root.

REGENTS REVIEW

1. In 1970, a deadly disease spread through corn crops in the United States. Scientists discovered that 80 percent of the corn contained the gene that made the plants more likely to be infected with the disease. This problem might have been avoided if the cornfields across the country had had more
    (1) large predators to control parasite populations
    (2) selective mutations
    (3) genetic diversity
    (4) breeding of infected plants

2. Growing exotic (nonnative) plant species in parks and gardens could lead directly to an increase in the
    (1) biodiversity of the autotrophs that feed on them
    (2) populations of native carnivores
    (3) competition between them and native producers
    (4) breeding between them and native herbivores

3. Scientists have been concerned about the reduction of shark populations due to overfishing off the east coast of the United States. Sharks feed on rays, which feed on scallops. Scallops feed on microscopic algae, which they filter from seawater. Without sharks, the rays consume and eliminate scallop beds, harming the scallop fishing industry. This situation demonstrates that
    (1) sharks are not important for the stability of this ecosystem
    (2) reducing the shark population increases the quantity of scallops that can be harvested
    (3) humans can upset ecosystem stability by removing species
    (4) humans improve ecosystem diversity by removing predators

The diagram represents the changes in an area over time.

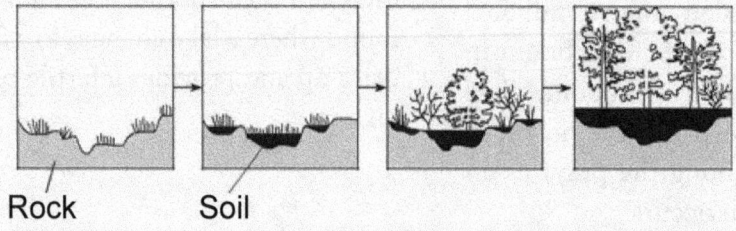

4. This series of changes in the area over hundreds of years is known as
    (1) evolution
    (2) feedback
    (3) ecological succession
    (4) direct harvesting

5) What is the primary source of energy for all the organisms in the ecosystem represented below?

(1) photosynthesis in the producers
(2) respiration in the heterotrophs
(3) light energy from the Sun
(4) minerals from the rocks

6. Shawangunk Grasslands National Wildlife Refuge has been developed from an abandoned airport to restore habitat for six species of birds that require an area rich in tall grasses. Workers must continually remove trees that are beginning to invade t the area as a result of
(1) direct harvesting
(2) genetic engineering
(3) evolutionary change
(4) ecological succession

7. Due to overfishing, the number of fish in the ocean could drastically decrease. This will cause
(1) an increase in the stability of the oceans
(2) an increase in the salt content of the oceans
(3) a decrease in the stability of the oceans
(4) a decrease in the oxygen available in the oceans

8. Over a long period of time, the stages represented in the diagram below were each present in a particular ecosystem.

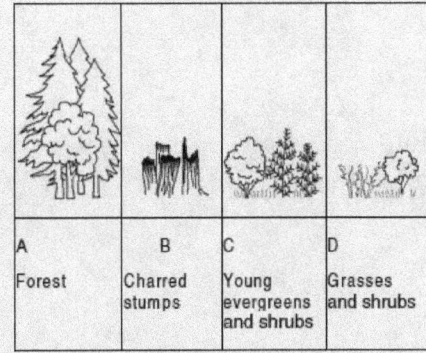

Living Environment Regents Review | 55

After a forest fire, what is the most likely order in which these stages appeared?
(1) D → C → A → B
(2) B → D → C → A
(3) A → B → C → D
(4) B → C → D → A

9. Which activity would reduce biodiversity in a forest ecosystem?
   (1) adding plants that are naturally resistant to insects
   (2) protecting wildflowers from logging activities
   (3) replacing harvested trees with young trees that are naturally found in the forest
   (4) clearing a large area and planting one species of hardwood tree that can be used for lumber

10. Environmentalists are hoping to protect endangered organisms by calling for a reduction in the use of pesticides, because loss of these organisms would
    (1) increase the mutation rate in plants
    (2) cause pesticides to become more toxic to insects
    (3) reduce biodiversity in various ecosystems
    (4) decrease the space and resources available to other organisms

11. Which process is represented in the diagram below?

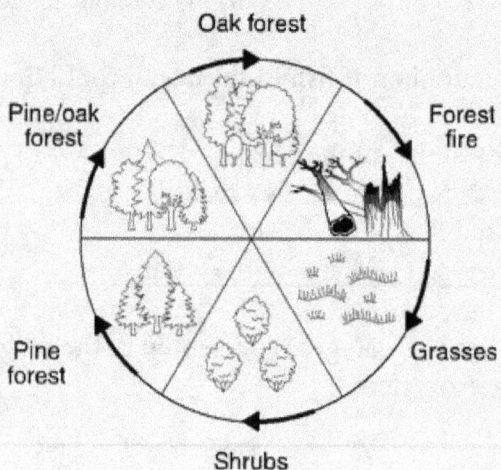

(1) energy flow
(2) biological evolution
(3) cellular communication
(4) ecological succession

CHAPTER 16
Human Impact on Ecosystems

73) Due to technological advancements in the past few hundred years, and the growth of the human population and resulting consumption, humans have begun to alter the ecosystem in profound ways. Scientists and environmentalists feel that we therefore need to become environmentally literate in order to ward off negative results from our choices. They claim that if we alter our environment in large ways, we can destroy the world we live in.

On Earth, we have two types of resources-renewable and non-renewable resources.

74) Renewable resources. Renewable resources are resources that can replenish themselves such as solar power and food. Yet even these resources may be stressed if we use them up at a rate where the species of food, for example, may not be able to replenish itself. For ex, if we consume bass at a rate faster than they multiply, the species becomes endangered and we are at risk of losing it.

75) Non-renewable resources. These are resources that have a finite quantity such as fossil fuels-gas, oil etc. If we deplete these resources we most likely will never have them again.

76) Soil formation and human usage-soil forms when rock breaks down after being exposed to the elements and by dead organic matter. This soil is maintained by roots of trees and plants. This soil is then the host for many organisms and decayed matter. The decay then gets transferred into plants that use the material of the deceased organism. This flow is called the Energy flow. Although nutrients can be recycled, energy CANNOT. The loss of energy into the atmosphere in the process of heat needs to be replaced by a different source like the sun which delivers energy into plants which starts the cycle anew. If people clear away trees and vegetation from the land and do not plant there again, the soil loses its anchors, becomes vulnerable and is liable to get washed away in the rain. If this happens we lose important minerals and organic material.

77) Water cycle. Water flows from the clouds in the form of rain. The rain that does not evaporate or go into the ground flows into bodies of water (lakes, rivers, oceans) which evaporate and go into the atmosphere and seed the forming clouds with water vapor. If pollutants are put into the atmosphere, the rain turns acidic and can kill plant life all over.

78) Many worried people fear that the world has/will have too many people on it and that humans and our ecosystem, the Earth, will reach carrying capacity. These worried people propose population control as a strategy in which to protect the environment and ourselves. Other strategies to protect our resources are the 3 R's:

- **reduce,** (for example: don't use the lights in your house when you don't really need to)
- **reuse** (for example: don't use paper plates, use dishes and reuse them many times),
- **recycle** don't throw things away, rather recycle used materials.

Pollution

Pollution is the harmful change in the water, soil, or air of a habitat which has a negative impact on the species of life living in that habitat.

Here are some of the ways humans alter the environment and harm it in the process:

- **Land clearing activities.** in order to set up human settlements or provide for the needs of humans, land is cleared for development. In the process, wildlife and sometimes whole ecosystems are adversely affected. Thus, while it is a positive thing to provide for humans-we need to be mindful of the environment and our impact on it.

- **Direct harvesting.** when a species is removed from its habitat or killed out, it is called direct harvesting. Direct harvesting can lead to the extinction (death) of a species. For ex. the passenger pigeon which numbered in the *billions* in the 1800's are now extinct!

- **Habitat destruction.** activities such as deforestation, (cutting down forests) kill off many species which then are unable to recover from the destruction of their habitat. For ex. the size of the rain forests are about half what they were 150 years ago. This loss of forest leads to a loss of biodiversity (which in many cases is a permanent loss as we lose the ability to find new cures from those species that were lost in the deforestation).

- **Imported species.** Many times, people unintentionally bring in new species into established habitats which lowers biodiversity. This happens because of increased competition with established species or because of the predator capacity of the new species which can cause irreversible damage to the existing species. To control these new pests is also a challenge. If one introduces a natural predator to this pest, it may itself become a new pest. Chemical controls don't either perform well being that it can harm other life in the area. The safest and most reliable way of pest control is using scented traps to capture and remove the pest.

REGENTS REVIEW

1. Increased human population growth usually results in
    (1) a decrease in the need for farming
    (2) a need for stronger environmental protection laws
    (3) lower levels of air and water pollution
    (4) an increase in natural wildlife habitats

2. The chart below summarizes the effect of commercial fishing on a local Atlantic cod population over an 9-year period.

Year	Number of commercial fishing boats	Estimated Population of Atlantic Cod (in thousands)
1995	4	14.0
1997	6	12.5
1999	12	11.5
2001	14	9.0
2003	17	4.5

   According to the chart, it can be concluded that
    (1) the number of fishing boats has less effect on the local cod population than pollution
    (2) more fishing boats make the cod population estimates more accurate
    (3) an increase in fishing boats has had a positive impact on cod population growth
    (4) commercial fishing is having a negative effect on the local cod population

3. A wetland provides a variety of services for an ecosystem, such as filtering pollutants from the water, allowing animals to lay eggs and reproduce, and producing fertile soils for plants. When humans build houses on wetland areas, they always
    (1) change this area so these processes can still take place
    (2) create new habitats for the wetland species
    (3) transport the wetland species to a new area
    (4) make changes that might not be reversible

According to the chart, it can be concluded that
(1) the number of fishing boats has less effect on the local cod population than pollution
(2) more fishing boats make the cod population estimates more accurate
(3) an increase in fishing boats has had a positive impact on cod population growth
(4) commercial fishing is having a negative effect on the local cod population

3. A wetland provides a variety of services for an ecosystem, such as filtering pollutants from the water, allowing animals to lay eggs and reproduce, and producing fertile soils for plants. When humans build houses on wetland areas, they always
    (1) change this area so these processes can still take place
    (2) create new habitats for the wetland species
    (3) transport the wetland species to a new area
    (4) make changes that might not be reversible

4. Which occurrence most likely led to the other three?
    (1) Human population growth reached 6.8 billion in 2010 and it continues to increase.
    (2) The number of African elephants has declined from 1.2 million in 1979 to about 20,000 today.
    (3) Approximately 6,500 gallons of oil were spilled into a river in Illinois after a pipeline broke.
    (4) At one time, rain forests covered 14 percent of Earth and today they cover only 6 percent.

5. A ski resort installed a wind turbine similar to those represented below to supply some of its energy needs.

6. This turbine was most likely installed because wind power is
    (1) renewable and does substantial damage to the atmosphere
    (2) renewable and does minimal damage to the atmosphere
    (3) nonrenewable and does substantial damage to the atmosphere
    (4) nonrenewable and does minimal damage to the atmosphere

6. As water flows downhill, its energy can be used to generate electricity. Later, this water may evaporate, fall as rain, and be used again to generate electricity in the same way. This explains why electricity generated with water is considered
    (1) a source of water pollution
    (2) a renewable form of energy
    (3) more expensive than nuclear energy
    (4) responsible for global warming

7. Scientists have found that although plants require light to carry on photosynthesis, very high levels of sunlight can kill some plants. This illustrates that many biochemical processes may occur
    (1) more rapidly when temperatures are very high
    (2) within a specific range of conditions
    (3) best in the absence of abiotic factors
    (4) even if homeostasis is disrupted

8. Some people see the benefit of wind energy as a clean alternative to fossil fuels for energy production. Others believe it is dangerous for migratory birds. These opinions best illustrate that decisions about alternate energy sources
    (1) will usually favor older methods of energy production over newer methods
    (2) must be made by weighing the risks and costs against the benefits
    (3) must be made by taking into account the present needs of the citizens without looking toward the future
    (4) should be the responsibility of each individual

9. Which farming practice causes the least harm to the environment?
    (1) using natural predators to reduce insect numbers
    (2) adding chemical fertilizers to all the crops in the area
    (3) planting the same crop for 1 year on all the fields in the area
    (4) planting the same crop in the same field each year for 10 years

CHAPTER 17
The Impact of Technology and Industrialization on the Environment

Industrialization

81) Many times, industrialization increases pollution as by-products of the manufacturing process. Industrialization also requires a lot of electricity which adds pollution to the atmosphere. This is due to the fact that electricity which fuels the industrialization is created at times through the burning of coal and other fossil fuels. For this reason, some countries have turned to nuclear powered power plants to provide for their energy needs. However, while nuclear power plants don't cause air or water pollution, they cause thermal pollution (see #84 below) and their radioactive wastes need to be disposed of safely. Furthermore, there can be nuclear meltdowns such as what happened in Japan's Fukoshima nuclear power plant and Chernobyl's power plant, destroying life in the immediate area for generations. Today, new energy sources are being sought after which provide clean sources of energy such as wind and solar energy.

82) Water pollution. Many industries dump their industrial wastes into bodies of water which increases agents of change in the water (abiotic factors of the environment) and harms the biotic balance of the habitat. For example, sewage dumped into the oceans acts as a fertilizer which causes blooms (increases) of algae. These algae eat up oxygen in the water which can eventually harm the livability of the water for fish and other wildlife.

83) Toxic Wastes. The waste produced by the factories have in many cases toxic elements. These wastes can cause great harm if they enter the water. Even if only small organisms sap up the toxic wastes, as the wastes move up the food chain they increase in concentration as they go. When they reach the top of the food chain, the amounts of toxins are so concentrated and great, they can many times cause great damage to those species and those that consume them.

84) Thermal pollution. Many nuclear power plants give off hot water into streams which raises the temperature of the stream. This causes a decrease in the dissolved oxygen in the stream given that warm water cannot hold as much dissolved oxygen as cold water can. This can cause species of fish to suffocate or move elsewhere for better waters.

85) Air pollution due to the burning of Fossil Fuels. Fuels such as gas and coal, which are conjectured to be formed from the breakdown of ancient fossils, release carbon dioxide and other potentially noxious gases into the air. If sulfur and nitrogen mix with rain, the rain becomes acidic and produces acid rain. This acid rain can damage plants if they are low enough on the Ph level. This also may make the plants more susceptible to disease or insects. If the acid rain runs into lakes and rivers and lowers the Ph levels of those lakes, it can kill off the organisms that require a more balanced Ph for survival. In addition, smog or the coloring of the atmosphere by pollutants–causes the air to turn brown or yellow when reacting to the rays of the sun, which can harm people with respiratory illnesses.

86) Global Warming. The average temperature of Earth has been rising over the last few decades (although the rise in temperature over the last 15 years has paused). Scientists speculate that this rise in temperature is due to the increase of certain gases in the atmosphere which traps the heat in the atmosphere. If the increase in greenhouse gases cause major climate change, then it can theoretically alter the world's food supply or melt the ice cap and flood some coastal areas around the globe. A major source for the increase in greenhouse gases is carbon dioxide produced by factories and cars. Planting more trees or pumping less carbon into the atmosphere can theoretically lower the impact of these greenhouse gases.

87) Ozone depletion. Due to the release of certain chemicals into the environment, the ozone layer that protects the Earth against ultraviolet rays are being destroyed which can cause these deadly rays to penetrate into the environment. If that happens there can be an increase in certain types of cancers which may kill off a number of organisms. This issue has been mostly resolved by removing the major ozone destroyer, CFC's, from refrigerants and aerosol cans.

88) Scientists and environmentalists feel that people need to be educated about the dangers of new technologies. They feel that people need to make informed and wise decision before allowing for the introduction of these technologies if they will irreparably harm the environment. Nations and individuals need to make informed and proper decisions about their environment.

REGENTS REVIEW

1. Some data suggest that the average global temperature will increase by 1°C–2°C by the year 2050. If this occurs, a major concern for humans would most likely be that
   (1) sea levels might rise enough to flood some coastal areas
   (2) long-term stability of the climate will benefit ecosystems
   (3) the availability of salt water for agricultural use will increase
   (4) the threat of extinction of land organisms will decrease

2. In which row in the chart below is a human action correctly paired with its environmental impact?

Row	Human Action	Environmental Impact
(1)	deforestation	increased biodiversity
(2)	population growth	increased number of species
(3)	industrialization	increased global temperature
(4)	overharvesting	increased mineral resources

3. An increase in the amount of ultraviolet light entering the atmosphere through holes in the ozone layer will most likely
   (1) reduce the rate of photosynthesis in fungi
   (2) result in rapid recycling of finite resources
   (3) prevent animal migration
   (4) cause an increase in the rate of certain mutations

4. One way humans can promote the survival of organisms in an ecosystem is to
   (1) decrease diversity in plant habitats
   (2) introduce new consumers to control autotrophs
   (3) release extra CO_2 into the atmosphere to help autotrophs
   (4) learn about the interactions of populations

5. Which action by humans could improve the quality of the air?
   (1) building homes that use only oil furnaces for heat
   (2) buying cars that get more miles per gallon of gasoline
   (3) increasing the number of coal-burning power plants that generate electricity
   (4) cutting down forests to clear land for factories

CHAPTER 18
Scientific Inquiry

89) Scientists advocate that people should develop a scientific literacy (knowledge of the scientific process) so that they are well prepared to distinguish between scientific truths and those that are not. For example, if a new study claims a certain find, one should ask how many studies where done (who funds the companies who did the studies to see if there is any conflict of interest), how big were the studies, were there control groups etc.). Thus, let us study the scientific method which will then teach us how to know what real science is made of.

90) The first step in any scientific study is observations using any of the five senses or tools to observe some phenomena. Better tools enable scientists to make better and more precise observations of the world. After an observation has been made, people make inferences, conclusions, or deductions based on their observations. Scientists, when studying something, try hard to keep assumptions about the matter observed to a minimum. Many assumptions can lead people to come to opinions which are biased as opposed to true objective facts.

91) Asking relevant questions about the observations made, leads scientists to develop a research plan which includes a hypothesis (or a possible explanation about the observations made). Yet before one develops a research plan, one needs to read through many books or do thorough research into the topic to see if others have already explored this issue. After you find that no one has looked into the topic, you create a hypothesis which in many cases is an if-then statement.

92) Designing experiments. After creating a hypothesis, one needs to develop an experiment (a test or a series of tests) that will either support or disprove the hypothesis. The object that you study is called the dependent variable. For example, if you are studying the effects of a growth hormone on plants, the dependent variable is the growth of plants after applying the growth hormone. The factors that might affect the dependent variable are called independent variables. (IV) Thus, continuing the previous example, the growth hormone and how much will be applied to the plants are called the IV. Next you need to establish a controlled experiment where the IV's are controlled so that one does not get false readings and results. For ex. if you don't start out with the same plants, how do you know that the results that were recorded were due to the placement of the growth hormone-maybe it was the different plants or soil? Sometimes you need a control group-where none of the items are tested and see the differences between the control group and the real group. Then you need to decide how many plants would support your hypothesis if an unknown IV was present and how many plants would be needed to eliminate any skewing of the results etc.

93) After creating a working experiment, one collects data. This collection must be done carefully to eliminate any unnecessary discrepancies. Then the data is collected and placed on a graph. There are 4 types of graphs a) pie or circle graph, b) bar graph (height matters), c) histogram (space in line matters) d) line graph. There are some basic rules about the rules of graphing. Rule 1) The vertical or y axis (or up and down) of the graph is reserved for the dependent variable. Rule 2) The x axis is reserved for the IV. Rule 3) the graphing must be done in equal increments.

94) After the results have been calibrated (carefully measure and placed) on the graph, a conclusion can be made. At this point a scientist has to make a determination if the results support or do not support the hypothesis. This is usually done using statistical models to see whether the outcome could be explained by chance. A model may be constructed to help explain the conclusions. For ex. The model for DNA helps explain how genes are passed down from one generation to the next. Further experimentation will either confirm or change the existing model.

95) After a successful experiment is run, further experimentation by other scientists should produce the same results. If they don't, then something is wrong. Scientists also review what was done and analyze the study's processes and findings. This process is called peer review. This process of peer review rests on the assumption that the methods of the experiment will be explained precisely (for if they weren't, they can misconstrue the results). If the reviewer sees that the study relied on a few inadequate samples or conclusions not supported by the experiment, they do not accept it.

REGENTS REVIEW

1. A community is trying to decide on the location for a new shopping center. Two possible locations have been proposed, with each location having some benefits and some problems. The proper approach to deciding the best location would be to
    (1) select the site that could hold the most stores
    (2) select the site that would be the least expensive to develop
    (3) compare the problems, but not the benefits
    (4) compare the trade-offs of building at either location

2. An experiment was designed to test whether students could squeeze a clothespin more times in 1 minute after resting or after exercising. What would be a hypothesis for the experiment?
    (1) Do students squeeze clothespins more often in 1 minute after exercising?
    (2) Can most students squeeze a clothespin more times after they rest?
    (3) Ten students who exercise before squeezing a clothespin squeezed it more times in 1 minute than ten students who rested first.
    (4) Students who rest before squeezing a clothespin will squeeze it fewer times in 1 minute than students who exercise beforehand.

Euglena are single-celled organisms that live in ponds. All euglena have chloroplasts and can make their own food. They can also take in food from the environment. The diagram below represents a euglena.

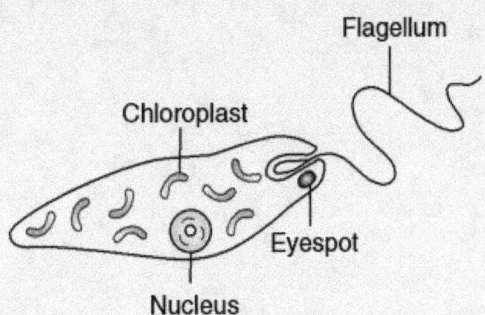

An experiment was set up to determine the effect of nitrates, a pollutant, on the number of chloroplasts present in euglena. Five tanks were set up, each with euglena and a different concentration of nitrate solution: 0%, 0.5%, 1.0%, 1.5%, and 2.0%.

The tanks were placed in a sunny location where each tank received the same amount of light.

3. Which statement is a possible hypothesis for this experiment that could be supported by the results of this experiment?
    (1) If the average number of chloroplasts in euglena decreases, will less nitrate be needed in each tank?
    (2) If the nitrate concentration is increased, then the euglena will have a lower average number of chloroplasts.
    (3) If the number of euglena in a tank increases, will more nitrates be produced?
    (4) If the nitrate concentration is decreased, then more light will reduce the average number of chloroplasts in euglena.

4. Which statement correctly identifies a variable in this experiment?
    (1) The independent variable is the concentration of nitrate solution used.
    (2) The dependent variable is the number of euglena placed in the tanks.
    (3) The independent variable is the amount of sunlight.
    (4) The dependent variable is the number of tanks used.

CHAPTER 19
Laboratory Skills

96) Measuring length is usually done using a metric ruler, a ruler which is calibrated in centimeters with millimeters in between. Millimeters are broken down under a microscope into micrometers. (10 millimeters equal 1 centimeter, 1000 micrometer equals 1 millimeter). Measuring volume is done using a graduated cylinder which when measuring liquids creates a meniscus (or a bend in the liquid) curving down. 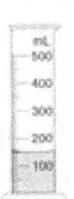 When measuring volume, one measures at the bottom of the curve. Measuring temperature is done using a thermometer which measures in Celsius. To measure mass, a Triple Beam Balance (a type of scale) is used which has 3 bars: a) a 500-gram bar divided into five equal parts, a) 100-gram bar divided into 10 equal parts and a 10-gram bar divided again into 10 equal parts. In modern labs, an electronic balance is used to measure mass (basically a scale). Make sure you subtract any added weight of protective paper on the balance before calibrating the mass of the object.

Microscope skills

97) Microscopes work by magnifying an object which makes an object appear bigger than it really is. There are two types of microscopes:

- **Compound microscope.** has one ocular lens (lens you look through) and one or more objective lens (lens that provides magnification). To get the strength of the lens, one needs to multiply the strength 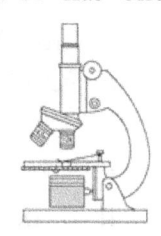 of the ocular lens by the objective lens in use to obtain the level of magnification. (Thus, if the ocular is 10x and the objective is 30x, then the magnification is 10 x 30=300.) It also has a light source that passes through the specimen and the level of light is controlled by the diaphragm. In order to get a better view of the specimen you are looking at, you can adjust the coarse adjustment which causes a large amount of adjustment and fine adjustment used to perfect the image.

Living Environment Regents Review | 69

- **Stereoscope.** A stereoscope has two lenses and an objective(s). Its lens usually has a low magnification but shows a three-dimensional image which is not reversed like it is in the compound microscope

Techniques for using microscopes

- Being that the compound microscope shows specimens backwards and upside down, if a specimen is moving to the upper right hand corner of the microscope you need to turn the slide to the lower left side.
- The field becomes darker as the magnification increases. Therefore you need to adjust the amount of light coming through the microscope in order to keep a good field of view.
- Since the field of view diminishes with higher magnification-one should center the object before viewing.
- Go from low power objectives to high power objectives and always view while adjusting. Be careful not to touch the slide in the process.
- If you don't want the specimen to shrivel and dry up, place a drop of water using an eye dropper (called a pipette) and place a coverslip (thin glass sheeting) using forceps (pliers for the lab) over a wet specimen which will keep it moist and prevent bubbling.
- To stain a specimen underneath a coverslip, place a drop of dye on one side of the specimen and place a paper towel on the other side. The paper towel will draw out the water underneath the coverslip and pull the dye across the specimen.
- Gel electrophoresis. Gel electrophoresis is a process where a gel is applied to a protein which then helps break apart the protein or DNA using electricity. Larger molecules go slower through the gel and therefore get separated from the smaller, faster molecules. This then helps scientists view parts of the proteins or DNA based on their size. The shapes formed by this process are highly individualized since everyone's DNA is different and thus it allows us sometimes to determine paternity or criminality.
- Chromatography. This technique is used for separating mixtures of molecules by placing some solvent on the edge of a piece of paper with the mixture on it and letting the solvent soak into the paper. As it soaks the paper, it pulls apart the parts of the mixture which have various amounts of attachments to the paper, with the less attracted parts going further, and the more attracted, slower parts staying close to the source.
- Stains and indicators. Dyes commonly used are methylene blue (used for staining parts of the nucleus) and iodine. An indicator is something that changes color when it comes in contact with certain items. Examples of this are Ph paper (which shows up in the presence of bases and acids) and Iodine (lugol's) solution which turns brown in the presence of starches. Many kits such as pregnancy kits and swimming pool kits use indicators to determine the presence of certain items in a solution.

A cell and some of its parts

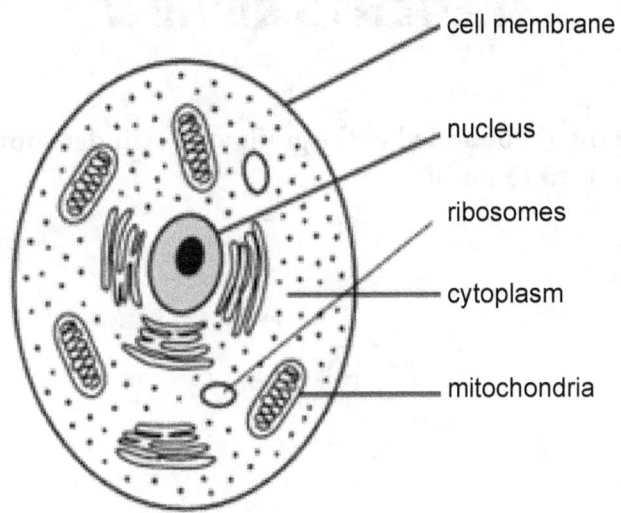

Dichotomous key: is a key used to break down two things which have similarities but also differences into clear categories. Always begin with the first thing mentioned in a dichotomous key and follow the line of reasoning. The following is an example of such a key.

1. 1a. This organism has an exoskeleton - go to question 2
   1b. This organism has an endoskeleton or no skeleton - go to question 3

2. 2a. This organism has thin black body and a red stripe on it's abdomen - go to question 4a.
   2b. This organism has a thick black body with large grey/brown abdomen - go to question 4b.

3. 3a. Organism dwells on land - go to question 5
   3b. Organism dwells in the ocean - go to question 6

4. 4a. Organism is called Latrodectus hasselti
   4b. Organism is called Atrax infensus

Lab tools:

- **Dissecting pan.** a pan resembling a frying pan with a waxy body in which a specimen is placed
- **Dissecting pin.** a pin with a "T" like top
- **Scalpel.** used to cut open specimens
- **Scissors.** also like a scalpel but also can be used to take out internal parts of an organism
- **Probe.** helps point out, pull apart, different parts of a specimen
- **Tweezers.** also used to lift out small parts
- **Safety goggles.** used to protect the eyes against accidental splashes and other lab hazards

Lab Safety Tips:

- Always heat tube facing away from you.
- Never heat up tube with stopper on
- If you spill the tube wash off immediately or seek medical guidance

Living Environment Regents Review | 71

REGENTS REVIEW

1. How much water should be added to the graduated cylinder shown below to increase the volume to 15 milliliters?

   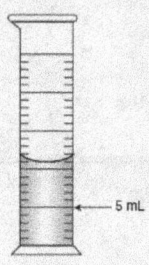

   (1) 11 mL (3) 3 mL
   (2) 10 mL (4) 4 mL

A diagram of the actual size of a peppered moth wingspan is shown below.

2. An estimated length of the wingspan could be
   (1) 3 centimeters (3) 3 milliliters
   (2) 3 grams   (4) 3 kilometers

An investigation was carried out to determine which of three antibacterial soaps is most effective. Four petri dishes labeled A, B, C, and D were set up. The same amount and type of bacteria was added to each dish. Next, 2 mL of a different brand of soap were added to dishes B, C, and D. Then, 2 mL of water were added to dish A, instead of soap. The dishes were incubated at 37°C for 24 hours. At the end of the investigation, the amount of bacteria in each dish was determined. Dish D had the least bacteria. It was concluded that the soap in dish D was the most effective soap to use against bacteria.

3. Which statement best describes the validity of this conclusion?
   (1) The conclusion is not valid since the same amount of bacteria was used in each dish.
   (2) The conclusion is valid since too small a sample of bacteria was used in this investigation.
   (3) The conclusion is valid since the amounts of bacteria were measured at the end of the investigation.
   (4) The conclusion might not be valid since the investigation was carried out only once.

4. In an experiment to test the effect of exercise on the number of times a clothespin can be squeezed in 1 minute, the dependent variable would be the
   (1) test subject
   (2) amount of exercise
   (3) number of squeezes
   (4) clothespin

In an experiment, students placed a dialysis bag containing 100 mL of a starch-water mixture in a beaker of water, as shown below. They left the setup until class the next day, when they removed the dialysis bag and measured the volume of the contents. They found that there were now 125 mL of the starch-water mixture.

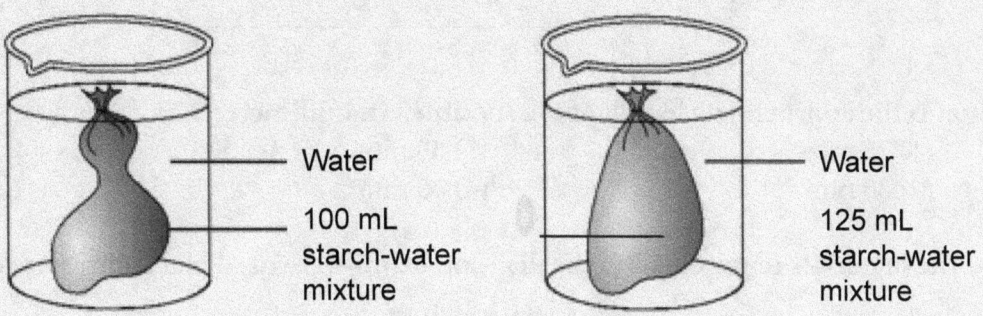

5. To measure the volume of the starch-water mixture in the dialysis bag, the students should have used a
   (1) meterstick
   (2) triple-beam balance
   (3) graduated cylinder
   (4) test tube

The diagram below represents the results of a laboratory procedure.

6. This procedure is used to
   (1) separate molecules in a liquid mixture
   (2) determine the rate of photosynthesis in plants
   (3) detect glucose in a solution
   (4) examine the gene sequences of organisms

DNA samples can be separated according to size using the technique of
(1) chromatography
(2) electrophoresis
(3) replication
(4) dissection

8. The diagram below represents the measurement of a biological specimen.

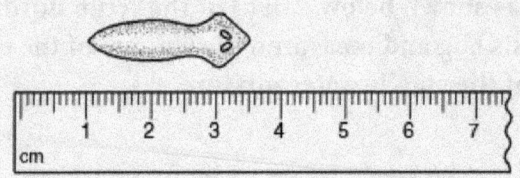

What is the approximate length of the specimen in millimeters?
(1) 25 mm
(2) 30 mm
(3) 35 mm
(4) 40 mm

9. The materials represented in the diagram below were used in a laboratory activity.

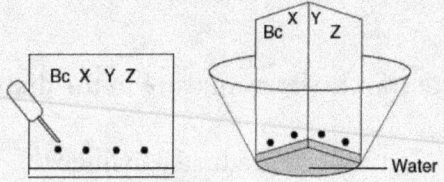

These materials were used to carry out the technique known as
(1) DNA staining
(2) genetic engineering
(3) paper chromatography
(4) glucose testing

10. A coverslip should be slowly lowered from a 45° angle onto a slide in order to
    (1) prevent the slide from being scratched
    (2) stop the loss of water from under the coverslip
    (3) ensure that the specimen being viewed will stay alive
    (4) reduce the formation of air bubbles

11. A substance is most likely to diffuse into a cell when
    (1) it is a large organic food molecule such as protein or starch
    (2) it is enclosed in an organelle such as a vacuole
    (3) the concentration of the substance is greater outside the cell than inside
    (4) the pH of the substance is greater than the pH of the cell

12. If a control group is not included in an experiment, it would be difficult to
    (1) formulate a hypothesis for the experiment
    (2) make observations about the experimental group
    (3) record data in a data table
    (4) draw a valid conclusion

The drawings below were made during a laboratory exercise in which a microscope was used to view slides of preserved protozoa. The microscope had a 10x eyepiece and two different objectives.

Organism A viewed with 10x objective   Organism B viewed with 40x objective

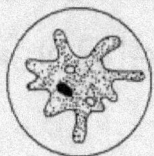
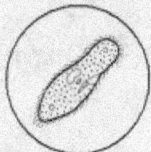

13. Which statement about the size of the organisms is correct?
    (1) Organism A is larger than organism B.
    (2) Organism B is larger than organism A.
    (3) Organisms A and B are both the same size.
    (4) The relative size of the organisms cannot be determined from the information given

A student performed a gel electrophoresis experiment. The results are represented in the diagram below.

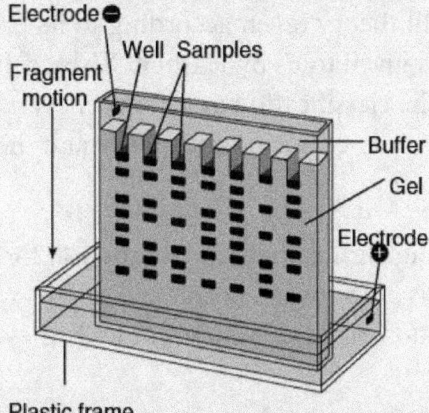

14. Compared to the fragments at the top of the gel, the fragments at the lower end are
    (1) larger, and move slower
    (2) larger, and move faster
    (3) smaller, and move faster
    (4) smaller, and move slower

CHAPTER 20
The Theory of Evolution

Disclaimer:
by Rav Chaim Yisroel Belsky zatza"l

Some time ago an idea was proposed which would explain the reason for the variety of species that we find in existence. It was theorized that the species came about by themselves by random selection and it was given the name Theory of Evolution. This became the cornerstone of non-believers in G-d. They tried to spread their ideas that the world came about by accident. So long as it was known as the Theory of Evolution it wasn't completely dangerous. In recent years, they began to label this material in terms that made it sound as if it was accepted as proven fact. This is the way of all non-scientists and fools. At first they reject belief in Hashem Yisbarach and then they begin to believe in themselves claiming that whatever drops into their omniscient mind can be claimed as factual. All the material under the heading "evolution" is still theory (even according to its proponents) and nothing else. To a believer in the teachings given to us by Hashem Yisbarach, claims and theories of this kind are to be disregarded. The classification given by believers in this theory as a branch of science is patently ridiculous; science means knowledge and there is nothing there based on any form of knowledge whatsoever.

We give you the main elements of this theoretical proposal for one reason, and one reason only- since the examination is given by governmental organs who chose to test students on it, despite the fact that it is a non-science, we present what they claim.

100) The Theory of Evolution says the following: life has evolved from simple organisms (single celled organisms) to complex organisms (with many systems working together) over billions of years. The theory says that at the start of life on Earth, life consisted of simple single celled organisms, but due to genetic mutations they evolved over time into complex organisms (like humans).

101) In support of this theory, scientists point to the fossil record which seems to show organisms growing in complexity over time. This fossil record spans geologic time and therefore used as proof of the Theory of Evolution.

102) Evolution does not say that all organisms will progress to higher states of complexity but rather it looks more like a bush; some branches go up and split off into new directions as they evolve while others just go to the side and die out. In the process called natural selection, individuals with positive mutations survive and those without those positive mutations die out. (see more later on) Those species that have this positive variation are said to have an adaptive value.

103) Scientists who advocate this theory have attempted to explain the changes through genetic mutation. Genetic mutation happens when a base in the DNA sequence changes due to random chance, events that cannot be predicted. Sometimes though, the mutations arise as a result of the organism being exposed to radiation or by being exposed to certain chemicals. For ex. survivors of the Chernobyl's nuclear meltdown were born with certain defects that arose when their parent's sex cells were exposed to radiation. Most mutations are harmful but a minute number are beneficial. If the mutations happen to be those that are passed down to the next generation, (like if the mutations are found in the gametes in multicellular organisms) then the next generation will be more suited for survival. For example, if a bear has black fur in the arctic he may not be a very good hunter since he will be seen by the animals he hunts and they will escape from him. If, however he has a mutation which turns his fur white, (like polar bears) then he will be able to blend into the environment and become a good hunter which will raise his chances of survival.

104) Here are some of the ways scientists say that evolution can express itself:

105) Structural changes. Scientists claim that many structural changes to the frames of organisms happened over time due to evolutionary forces. Thus, say scientists, many animals have similarities since they may have evolved from a common ancestor. Additionally, claim scientists, some structures on organisms that are no longer in use point to an evolutionary "dead end".

106) Functional Changes. are changes in actions of certain cells that make animals adapt better. For example, how much electricity is produced by the organism. Human muscles emit tiny electrical impulses while eels produce massive amounts of energy which stuns or kills its prey. Thus, for eels, functional changes in muscles have led to its survivability.

107) Behavioral changes: are evolutionary changes in behavior which are beneficial. For ex. fighting among male animals for females. This behavior allows for the healthiest male to reproduce and thus increase the chances of survival of the species.

108) Importance of variation: due to genetic changes, species develop greater variation in their species. If a species has variation, then if that species is confronted by a challenge to its survival, then it has a greater chance of surviving due to that variation.

109) Rate of evolutionary change: Some species show little change while others lots of change. Generally speaking, species that live and reproduce over a short period of time, rapidly evolve while others that live long lives change very slowly. For example, bacteria, which reproduce very quickly, if attacked by antibiotics may develop a resistance to the antibiotics due to a process of natural selection. In this case, bacteria which mutates in a positive way and develops an immunity against the antibiotics will survive and reproduce and eventually make the antibiotics ineffective. Another example are insects and insecticides. Insects have also evolved and have become resistant to certain insecticides.

110) Extinction: When a species cannot keep up, or adapt, with the changes occurring in its environment and has little genetic variety, it may face extinction (death). Thus, most animals that have lived in the past have disappeared due to the fact that they could not adapt to the new environment.

REGENTS REVIEW

The diagram below represents the bone arrangements in the front limbs of three different species of mammals.

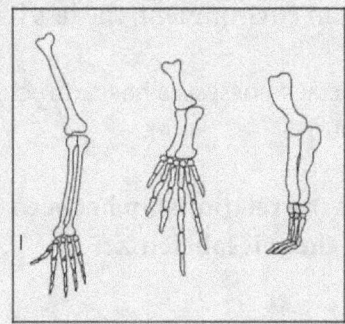

1. The similarities and differences in these limbs suggest that all three species developed from the same ancestor, but
    (1) produced different numbers of offspring
    (2) lived in different time periods
    (3) adapted to different habitats
    (4) migrated to similar habitats

2. People have been warned about the dangers of excessive exposure to radiation during certain medical procedures. The most likely reason for this warning is that radiation exposure might
    (1) result in gene mutations and uncontrolled cell growth
    (2) cause the rejection of transplanted organs
    (3) increase body temperature by two to five degrees
    (4) prevent the transport of materials into cells

The graph below shows the changes in the number of individuals in a population who have a specific trait.

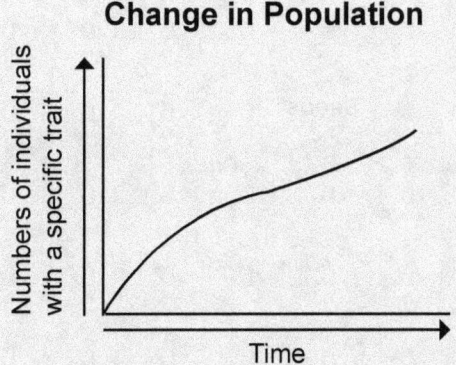

3. Which statement concerning this trait is a valid inference?
   (1) As tme passed, an increasing number of individuals with this trait survived and reproduced.
   (2) Individuals can acquire new survival characteristics over time and pass them on to their offspring.
   (3) The longer a species is in an environment, the less likely it is that mutations will occur within the species.
   (4) The number of traits a species possesses has a direct relationship to the amount of time the species will exist.

4. The diagram below represents the relationship between natural selection and variation. The arrow between them is labeled X.

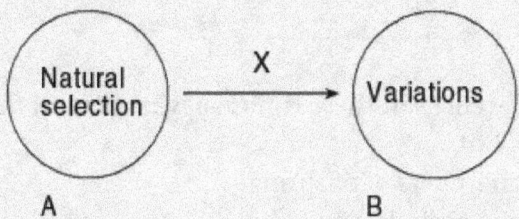

Which phrase best indicates the meaning of the arrow labeled X?
   (1) is dependant on
   (2) increases the rate of
   (3) decreases the rate of
   (4) is independant of

Finches on the Galapagos Islands are thought to have originated from South America and *supposedly* have evolved into new species over the last 10,000 years. Some of this evolution is represented in the diagram below.

**Darwin's Finches
Adaptive Radiation**

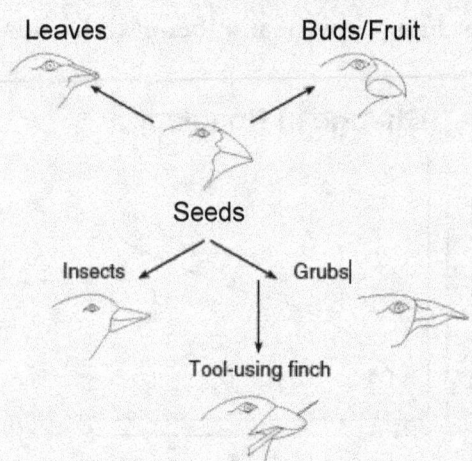

5. The success of the finches on the Galapagos was most likely due to the
   (1) large numbers of other birds competing for food
   (2) mutations occurring in every offspring
   (3) birds occupying the same island
   (4) birds adapting to different niches

6. The seed-eating finch was most likely the
   (1) largest finch
   (2) common ancestor
   (3) parent of the other finches
   (4) most successful

7. In order for a species to evolve, it must be able to
   (1) consume a large quantity of food
   (2) reproduce successfully
   (3) maintain a constant body temperature
   (4) be domesticated

8. A population of white moths lives in a forest near a factory. This factory burns coal and pollutes the air with black dust. Over time, this dust has settled on the trees in the area, making them darker in color. This could result in
   (1) an increase in the white moth population
   (2) a decrease in the white moth population
   (3) an increase in the number of trees in the area
   (4) a decrease in the air pollution affecting the area

9. The crucian carp, a Scandinavian fish, thrives in shallow ponds that freeze over during winter. While other creatures in the pond die from lack of oxygen, these carp are able to obtain energy through a biochemical pathway that does not require oxygen. This characteristic is an example of a
   (1) feedback mechanism common to carnivores that inhabit shallow pond ecosystems
   (2) favorable adaptive trait that has led to increased survival
   (3) stage of succession that leads to a new community
   (4) gene mutation that occurred because carp need to survive to maintain ecological stability

10. Examination of ancient rock layers at a certain location reveals many different fossils. Which conclusion can be drawn concerning the species that formed these fossils?
    (1) Only the predators are still present.
    (2) Many of them are now extinct.
    (3) They produced offspring that were all genetically identical.
    (4) They had no variations due to mutations.

The diagram below represents some changes that took place in a bacterial population recently exposed to an antibiotic.

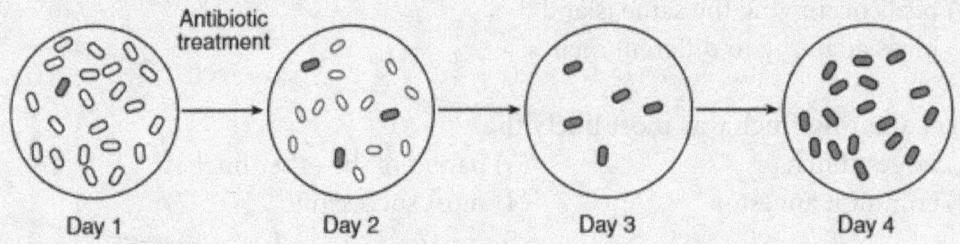

11. Which statement would best explain the presence of bacteria on day 4?
    (1) A bacterial population cannot survive exposure to antibiotics.
    (2) This bacterial population cannot survive exposure to this antibiotic.
    (3) Bacteria can change whenever it is necessary to survive antibiotic treatment.
    (4) Some of the bacterial population was resistant to this antibiotic.

Yes, This Big Lizard is Pink

A new study from the University of Rome Tor Vergata shows that a rare strawberry-tinted land iguana [rosada iguana] in the Galapagos Islands is genetically distinct from other iguanas there, having (supposedly) diverged from them more than five million years ago as the archipelago [a group of islands] formed. The rosada iguana—which escaped Darwin's notice—was discovered only recently, largely because it lives on the desolate slopes of an active volcano

12. According to information in the article, it is most likely that
    (1) the ancestors of this iguana were (supposedly) separated from ancestors of other Galapagos iguanas millions of years ago and adapted to different environments
    (2) the ancestors of this iguana came from the mainland of South America (supposedly) millions of years ago and needed to adapt to the conditions of the Galapagos
    (3) gases released from an active volcano caused ancestral iguanas to mutate so they could adapt to the hot, dry environment near the volcano
    (4) it is a color variation of the same species of iguana that lives elsewhere on the island, and it was not discovered because it blended in with its environment near the volcano

13. Several of the Galapagos Islands are inhabited by grasshoppers, beetles, flies, bees, and butterflies. Finches that feed on these consumers would have beaks adapted for
    (1) pobing, only
    (2) probing or grasping
    (3) crushing or probing
    (4) parrotlike feeding or grasping

14. Parrots are tropical birds. However, in some areas of New York City, some parrots have been able to survive outdoors year-round. These parrots survive, while most others cannot, due to
    (1) overproduction of offspring
    (2) extinction of previous species
    (3) asexual reproduction of parrots with a mutation
    (4) a variation that allows these parrots to live in colder climates

The table below shows adaptations in two organisms.

Environmental Adaptations

Organism	Environment	Adaptation
desert rat	hot and dry	comes out of burrow only at night
Arctic poppy plant	cold and windy	grows low to ground next to rocks

15. The presence of these adaptations is most likely the result of
    (1) reproductive technology
    (2) natural selection
    (3) asexual reproduction
    (4) human interference

16. Characteristics that are harmful to a species tend to decrease in frequency from generation to generation because these characteristics usually
    (1) have a high survival value for the species
    (2) have a low survival value for the species
    (3) are inherited by more individuals
    (4) affect only the older members of the population

17. Many scientists conjecture that billions of years ago, life on Earth began with
    (1) simple, single-celled organisms
    (2) simple, multicellular organisms
    (3) complex, single-celled organisms
    (4) complex, multicellular organisms

18. Certain chemicals, such as cytochrome C, are found within cells of all living organisms. The biochemical structure of cytochrome C in ground finches and in tree finches is very similar. This suggests that tree finches and ground finches have
    (1) identical DNA
    (2) a common ancestor
    (3) evolved at the same time
    (4) the same nesting site

19. Which characteristic is necessary for natural selection to occur in a species?
    (1) stability
    (2) variation
    (3) complex cellular organization
    (4) a very low mutation rate

20. The evolutionary pathways of several species are represented in the diagram below.

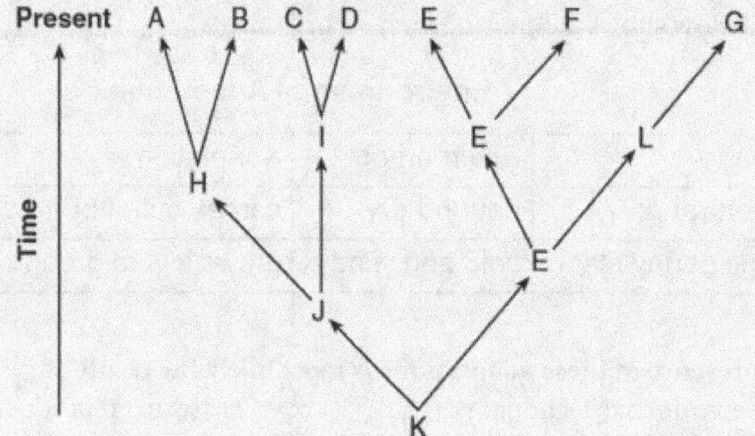

Which species was best adapted for survival in changing environmental conditions?
    (1) A   (3) K
    (2) E   (4) L

Answer Key

Chapter 1: Life Processes
1) **Answer:** 4 see # 1d where it says all living things reproduce
2) **Answer:** 3 see # 1c where it discusses homeostasis
3) **Answer:** 2 see # 1c where it discusses homeostasis

Chapter 2: Cells and their parts
1) **Answer:** 3 see # 7 and #9 for info on Nucleus and Ribosome
2) **Answer:** 2 see # 12 and 13 for info on Cell Membrane and diffusion
3) **Answer:** 3 see # 13 and # 14 for difference between active transport and diffusion-since diffusion is where there is a higher concentration outside the cell and here it is not-then it must be active transport.
4) **Answer:** 3 see # 15 where it discusses digestion and synthesis as opposite processes
5) **Answer:** 2 see # 7 for more info on these three components
6) **Answer:** 4 see # 7 for more info about what makes differences between creatures
7) **Answer:** 2 see # 7 for the importance of genes in the creation of various parts of animals
8) **Answer:** 3 see # 13 and 14 for info about active transport
9) **Answer:** 3 see # 7 about the nucleus
10) **Answer:** 3 see # 10 and 11 about these two organelles.
11) **Answer:** 1 see # 7 about the role of genes in living organisms. Being that cells create functionality from their genes through protein synthesis then it is this process that is most affected by these experiments.
12) **Answer:** 3 being that only the round balls fit into cell 1 this must be the answer since hormones must be able to bind to a site on the cell in order to make it functional
13) **Answer:** 1 see # 7 about the role of bases such as A an T

Chapter 3: Multicellular systems
1) **Answer:** 4 see # 17 for more info on Glucose
2) **Answer:** 1 see # 22 for more info on the similar roles that the nervous and endocrine systems play
3) **Answer:** 3 see # 17 for info how energy is released from molecules
4) **Answer:** 1 see # 17 and # 13 for more info about water coming into the cell through diffusion alone

Living Environment Regents Review | 85

5) **Answer**: 1 see # 12 and # 18 above. Just as the cell membrane transfers wastes and food through itself, so too do the lungs draw in air and exhale wastes-CO_2

6) **Answer**: 2 see note above

Chapter 4: Cell Respiration in Plants and Animals

1) **Answer: 1** see # 28 for more on how chloroplasts provide energy for plants

2) **Answer: 2** see # 30 and 31 for more on ATP

3) **Answer: 1** see # 30 for more on metabolic wastes

4) **Answer: 1** see note above

5) **Answer: 3** see # 29 for more on how Enzymes are used to cut DNA

6) **Answer: 2** see # 28. Being that energy is converted into molecules (chemical energy) and carbon is an organic molecule (see entry # 4), then this must be the answer.

7) **Answer: 3** see # 28 for more on how humans exhale carbon dioxide and inhale oxygen while plants do the opposite.

Chapter 5: Enzymes

1) **Answer: 2** see # 32 c for Ph change and the way it affects enzymes

2) **Answer**: 1 see #32 a for importance of shape in enzymes

3) **Answer**: 1 as can be seen the enzyme is the outside case which binds the two pieces of matter together for some kind of biological function. Thus, if the enzyme has an increase in temperature, one can expect a change in enzyme function (see # 32c)

4) **Answer**: 3 as is evident from the graph-the middle above 35 degrees produces the highest number of bubbles showing the greatest amount of enzyme activity.

Chapter 6: Homeostasis

1) **Answer**: 1 see # 33 for more on leaf pores

2) **Answer**: 4 this is part of the process of homeostasis-the more oxygen required by the body the more a person breathes see #36 for more

3) **Answer**: 4 obviously organelles being that it is a single celled organism

Chapter 7: Disease and Homeostasis

1) **Answer**: 4 See #40 last bullet where it discusses allergies

2) **Answer**: see # 40 second to last bullet where it discusses AIDS

3) **Answer**: 1 see # 40 where it discusses antigens and antibodies

4) **Answer**: 3 see # 40 last bullet about allergic reactions

Chapter 8: Reproduction

1) **Answer**: 2 see # 42 and # 50 about changes in sex cells and inheritance

2) **Answer**; 2 see # 44 for more about mitosis

3) **Answer**: 3 see # 41 for more about asexual reproduction

4) **Answer**: 2 see # 44 for more on mitosis-the choices are poor but mitosis is the best choice

5) **Answer**: 3 see # 44 for more on fertilization and the formation

of a zygote. This drawing shows the beginning stages of fertilization with the formation of the zygote and then differentiation

6) **Answer**: 4 see # 46 for more about cloning
7) **Answer**: 1 see # 46 for more on testosterone and its role in the male reproduction
8) **Answer**: 2 being that only # 2 has been born from sexual reproduction which involves two parents-therefore this must be the only answer see # 41-42 for more
9) **Answer**: 2 since there is both female and male that would not be a clone since they contain different genes
10) **Answer**: 2 see # 45 for more on the role of the placenta
11) **Answer**: 3 since the A is between the zygote and young squirrels that means that it is growing from a zygote which happens with mitosis
12) **Answer**: 3 being that it was produced from the mother's milk that means it is in the mother's genes and therefore must have been inserted into the goat's genes (see # 42, 50)
13) **Answer**: 1 see # 24 and 42 about testes and gametes
14) **Answer**: 1 see # 45 for more about environmental effects on a baby's development
15) **Answer**: 2 see # 44 and 51 for process of expressing genes
16) **Answer**: 3 see # 43 for more about recombination
17) **Answer**: 2 being that there is the process of cloning (essentially although the bacteria is splitting and not being done in the lab-essentially it is really a form of cloning

Chapter 9: DNA Action and Replication

1) **Answer**: 3 see # 48 about RNA synthesis. This shows that process as the DNA unfolds and the pieces of genetic code are read.
2) **Answer**: 1 see # 48 about the process that creates cell parts of all types which are created by the folding of proteins into certain shapes which then create working cell parts
3) **Answer**: 2 since the creation of parts of the cell ultimately rely on the DNA code, if one base of a gene is changed then a different form of the cell will be created.
4) **Answer**: 1 see # 48 as is explained there-the ribosomes are the place where proteins are synthesized into various parts of a cell.
5) Answer: 3 see # 48 and # 2 before

Chapter 10: Mutations and Individuality

1) **Answer**: 3 see # 51 about how environment can turn on certain genes
2) **Answer**: 3 see # 49 more about heredity
3) **Answer**: 1 DNA, which is the codes for all cell parts and functions do this in regard for all parts including the molecules that receive communications.

4) **Answer**: 1 see # 51 being that the environment changed, certain genetic expressions were affected
5) **Answer**: 3 see # 50 for more on mutations
6) **Answer**: 1 if you look at the two sides of the arrow you see one has a whole section (ACC) that has been deleted in the right side thus the answer is deletion
7) **Answer**: 3 see # 51 for more about the effects of environment on gene
8) **Answer**: 3 see # 50 for more how certain mutations are passed down hereditarily
9) **Answer**: 4 see # 50 being that the only one that has no mutation in the sex cells is the 4th then this one is the most unlikely one to pass down the mutation
10) **Answer**: 1 being that this is not a mutation in the gametes therefore it will only be reproduced by that cell
11) **Answer**: 3 see # 50 more about the role of environment in creating mutations

Chapter 11: Genetic Engineering and Biotechnology
1) **Answer**: 4 see # 52 for more on selective breeding
2) **Answer**: 4 see # 53 for more on genetic engineering
3) **Answer**: 2 see # 53 for more on genetic engineering
4) **Answer**: 1 see # 52 for more on selective breeding
5) **Answer**: 4 see # 52 for more on selective breeding. Being that this choice is the only one that does not require lab work it must be the correct choice

Chapter 12: Ecology
1) **Answer**: 2 see # 61 for more on carrying capacity
2) **Answer**: 4 see # 61 for more on predators and prey
3) **Answer**:
— Disease killed large numbers of the moose.
— The moose population overgrazed its habitat, resulting in starvation.
— The moose population exceeded the carrying capacity of the environment.
— overhunting by wolves
— severe winter
4) **Answer**: 2 in order for there to be any kind of stability the predators and prey need to have a relation and dependence on each other
5) **Answer**: 1 see # 58(biosphere), 55(ecosystem), and 58(population) in that order
6) **Answer**: 4 being that climate will determine what type of species will be able to live there
7) **Answer**: 2 see # 11 for the role of chlorophyll and # 56 for the sun being an abiotic factor
8) **Answer**: 2 being that some plants thrive totally under water while some partially submerged and others almost completely exposed-this shows that the growth and survival depends on the physical conditions where they find themselves.

Chapter 13: Relationships in an Ecosystem
1) **Answer**: 4 see # 64 for more on autotrophs. Being that # 1 is the

largest one in the group, and autotrophs like algae and the like are at the bottom of the food chain, therefore they are the greatest source of energy

2) **Answer**: 3 see # 66 for more on parasites and # 65 and 69 for more on decomposers

3) **Answer**: 1 being that decomposers break down organisms after they had died (see # 65 and 69), and A takes from all three other species-this must be the correct answer

4) **Answer**: 2 although all the choices are possible, the one that would be the least disruptive and easiest to implement is to regulate the hunting of sea otters which would allow for some hunting but cap its use

5) **Answer**: 4 while all the others are acting in some capacity as a keystone species, # 4 shows the zebra mussels decimating the biodiversity of the area.

6) **Answer**: 2 see the passage where the feeding relationships are clearly shown

7) **Answer**: 4 it cannot be choice b because choice A gets its energy from the sun choice c don't get their energy from d rather from b and choice A are autorophs not herbivores. Thus, the only choice is 4

8) **Answer**: 1 environmental factors are the only ones that make sense here being that they are not producers, rely (dependent) on others, and they are limited by natural predators

9) **Answer**: 4 see # 59 for more on competition

10) **Answer**: 1 since a food chain represents what consumes what, biotic (other living creatures-see # 55) matter would most likely be represented

11) **Answer**: 1 see # 65 for more on decomposers. Being that mushrooms are a fungus, they absorb the nutrients from organic matter acting like a decomposer

12) **Answer**: 4 see # 66 for producers-those that produce the food-grass in this case and consumers-those that eat the food-deer in this case

13) **Answer**: 3 see # 66 again regarding consumers and producers. Being that there are more consumers than producers, the consumers will soon see an unstable environment

14) **Answer**: 4 see # 64 for more on Autotrophs and heterotrophs

15) **Answer**: 3 see # 66 for more on parasites and hosts

16) **Answer**: 2 being that the grasses were being eaten by the elk and the elk had no natural predators the elk population exploded. Therefore, to bring back down the manageable elk population, wolves were reintroduced.

17) **Answer**: 3 simply being that scavengers ate the remains of the dead elk the scavenger population increased. See # 66 for more on scavengers

Chapter 14: Energy Recycling

1) **Answer**: 1 see # 65 and # 69 for more on decomposers

Chapter 15: Biodiversity and Environmental changes

1) **Answer**: 3 see # 70 for more on biodiversity
2) **Answer**: 3 see # 71 for more about this phenomenon
3) **Answer**: 3 self-evident-being that we fished them-we are causing a disruption in the ecosystem
4) **Answer**: 3 see # 71 for more on ecological succession
5) **Answer**: 3 the sun is the primary source of energy on Earth going into plants which the animals eat and which ultimately provide energy to all living creatures.
6) **Answer**: 4 see # 71 for more on ecological succession
7) **Answer**: 3 see # 70 for more on the loss of biodiversity which leads to a lack of stability
8) **Answer**: 2 see # 71 for more on ecological succession shown in the picture
9) **Answer**: 4 see # 70 for more on biodiversity
10) **Answer**: 3 because the animals are endangered, with their elimination, biodiversity will be affected. See also # 79 and Chapter 17
11) **Answer**: 4 see # 71 for more on ecological succession

Chapter 16: Human Impact on Ecosystems

1) **Answer**: 2 this one is the only one that makes sense for with more people the need for more farming is greater and so does pollution increase with less space for wildlife
2) **Answer**: 4 as can be seen as the more fishing boats catching fish, the cod are declining
3) **Answer**: 4 self-understood being that the rest don't happen-
4) **Answer**: 1 because of human population, rainforests have disappeared, elephants have declined, and oil spills take place
5) **Answer**: 2 wind power is renewable see #74-75 being that it always blows and doesn't run out and does minimal damage to the environment
6) **Answer**: 2 see # 74 for more about renewable energy
7) **Answer**: 2 being that the conditions have to be right-if they are too high (such as what happens in pollution) life can be harmed
8) **Answer**: 2 that is what is said in the essay, one has to weigh the risks and costs of using technology to see weigh the risks and costs of using the technology
9) **Answer**: 1 see bullet # 3 of # 80

Chapter 17: The Impact of Technology and Industrialization

1) **Answer**: 1 see # 86 about the fears associated with global warming
2) **Answer**: 3 see # 86 again for info on global warming and its causes
3) **Answer**: 4 see # 87 for more on the dangers of ultraviolet light caused by ozone depletion
4) **Answer**: 4 the only one that makes sense
5) **Answer**: 2 by buying more fuel-efficient cars we will be pro-

ducing less emissions and thus cleaner air

Chapter 18: Scientific Inquiry

1) **Answer**: 4 obvious-if you only look at the benefits you aren't looking at the whole picture
2) **Answer**: 4 see # 91 for more on hypothesis. This choice reflects what a hypothesis (a possible explanation) is
3) **Answer**: 2 being that we are testing the effects of nitrates on euglena then a possible hypothesis is that the increase of nitrates will decrease the chloroplasts
4) **Answer**: 1 see # 92 for more on the independent variable

Chapter 19: Laboratory Skills

1) **Answer**: 4 being that the meniscus is on about 11 therefore that's where we begin measuring from (see # 96 for more)
2) **Answer**: 1 being that centimeters is the only measurement that makes sense (a moth is not kilometers wide) and milliliters and grams are not measurements of length
3) **Answer**: 4 see # 95 about further experimentation needed to prove the original results
4) **Answer**: 3 see # 92 about dependent variables
5) **Answer**: 3 see # 96 more about graduated cylinder-all the others don't fit here
6) **Answer**: 1 see # 97 and the bullet on chromatography
7) **Answer**: 2 see # 97 and the bullet about gel electrophoresis
8) **Answer**: 1 as you see-there are 5 millimeters in a centimeter and it goes from 1 to approx. 3.5 centimeters and a drop more which is about 25 millimeters
9) **Answer**: 3 see # 97 and the bullet on chromatography-in the diagram on the left the item were used to separate the materials and then they are placed (on the diagram on the right side) in their respective places
10) **Answer**: 4 see # 97 and the bullet discussing the coverslip
11) **Answer**: 4 see # 92 about control group
12) **Answer**: 1 being that you get the same size with 10x and 40x in the viewer that means that organism A is bigger than organism A
13) **Answer**: 3 since the items are placed in from the top-the ones on the bottom are smaller and faster and therefore go farther

Chapter 20: Evolution

1) **Answer**: 3 being that they have different structures the reason given is that these animals inhabit different habitats and therefore the changes
2) **Answer**: 1 see # 103 about the dangers of radiation
3) **Answer**: 1 as animals reproduce with one each other the trait spreads among the population
4) **Answer**: 1 natural selection is dependent on variations which allows one species to survive while the one without the adaption to die out. See # 102
5) **Answer**: 4 by adapting different niches the birds have a greater

chance of survival
6) **Answer**: 2 as you can see the arrows pointing out from it
7) **Answer**: 2 self-understood
8) **Answer**: 2 as the dirt makes the trees darker, the moths that inhabit those trees are less camouflaged and more exposed making them vulnerable to prey which will reduce their population
9) **Answer**: 2 see # 102 for more on positive adaptations
10) **Answer**: 2 being that different fossils are found in different layers tells us that those on the lower layers died out being that they aren't found on the upper layers
11) **Answer**: 4 being that dark color went from a single specimen to the whole colony that means that it was resistant to the bacteria leading to its survival
12) **Answer**: 1 as it is simply stated in the paragraph "rosada iguana]... is genetically distinct from other iguanas there, having (*supposedly*) **diverged** from them more than five million years ago as the archipelago [a group of islands] formed."
13) **Answer**: 2 probing for grasshoppers and beetles while grasping for the above and others
14) **Answer**: 4 see 3 102, 105, for more on adaptions
15) **Answer**: 2 both species have adapted to their environment
16) **Answer**; 2 being that they are harmful they eventually die out
17) **Answer**: 1 see # 100
18) **Answer**: 2 self-understood-that is why they both have similar cytochrome c
19) **Answer**: 2 see question # 4 above
20) **Answer**: 2 since A made it all the way to the present it has the greatest ability to survive

www.ingramcontent.com/pod-product-compliance
Lightning Source LLC
Chambersburg PA
CBHW051754100526
44591CB00017B/2699